THE UNITY AND DISUNITY
OF THE CHURCH

PATHWAY BOOKS

All Ye That Labor   by Lester DeKoster

The Pattern of Authority   by Bernard Ramm

When the Time Had Fully Come
        by Herman N. Ridderbos

Is There a Conflict Between Genesis 1 and Natural Science?
        by Nicolaas H. Ridderbos

Man in Nature and in Grace   by Stuart Barton Babbage

Archaeology and the Old Testament   by J. A. Thompson

Out of the Earth (Archaeology and the N. T.)
        by E. M. Blaiklock

Sacramental Teaching and Practice in the Reformation Churches   by G. W. Bromiley

Recent Developments in Roman Catholic Thought
        by G. C. Berkouwer

The Origin and Transmission of the New Testament
        by L. D. Twilley

Evangelical Responsibility in Contemporary Theology
        by Carl F. H. Henry

Who Wrote Isaiah?   by Edward J. Young

Archaeology and the Pre-Christian Centuries
        by J. A. Thompson

BIOGRAPHICAL NOTE

DR. G. W. BROMILEY recently joined the Fuller Theological Seminary faculty as professor of Church History and Historical Theology. For the past seven years he lectured at the Postgraduate School of Theology at New College in Edinburgh, Scotland, while serving as rector of the St. Thomas Church. Dr. Bromiley is the author of a distinguished biography, *Thomas Cranmer: Reformer and Theologian;* a short introduction to Christian ethics, *Reasonable Service;* a study of baptism entitled, *Baptism and the Anglican Reformers;* and other books. He contributed the article on "Authority of Scripture" in *The New Bible Commentary* and he regularly writes articles and book reviews for theological journals. He is a Contributing Editor to *Christianity Today.* He holds the B.A. degree from Emmanuel College in Cambridge and the Ph.D. and Litt. D. degrees from the University of Edinburgh. From 1946 to 1951 he was lecturer and vice-principal at Tyndale Hall, Bristol.

The Unity and Disunity
of the Church

BY

G. W. Bromiley, Ph.D., D. Litt.

WM. B. EERDMANS PUBLISHING COMPANY

GRAND RAPIDS, MICHIGAN

INTRODUCTION

ONE OF THE CONCERNS which has been laid upon the churches during the past decades is that of unity. It has grown not merely from the liberal emphasis upon brotherhood but from the spiritual and practical problems of disunity as they have found particular emphasis on the mission field and in face of modern aspostasy. Nor is it merely a tinkering with practical proposals for unification. Quite apart from schemes which have been carried into effect, there is a deep and prolonged examination of unity from the ultimate biblical and theological standpoint which must underlie all concrete schemes if they are to be a genuine contribution to unity.

The upsurge of this movement poses the inescapable question to all Christians what must be their attitude to it. They may not approve the detailed forms which it takes. They may see many mistakes in the action of a body like the World Council of Churches. They may distrust ecclesiastical plans or deplore the ignoring of various sections of opinion. They may feel that too much time is wasted with talk of unity when various steps which could be taken are not taken, and others are not necessary in any case. But it cannot be denied that real disunity, even for what seems to be the best of reasons, is a definite evil in the church. The movement for unity is thus to be applauded in principle. And while it is right that there should be firm but good-tempered criticism of wrong ideas and courses, the supreme task is the positive one of guiding it, if possible, to a right understanding and therefore to correct and fruitful action.

In the present study the task is attempted of pointing to the true nature of the church's unity, and drawing from this the concrete task of the churches in relation to this question.

The detailed outworking of the rich themes and complicated issues involved is naturally impossible in the course of a book of this length. Yet it is hoped that enough will be said both to indicate where the real center of unity is to be found, to outline the pattern which it must assume in the church, and to show the ways in which it can be given concretion.

By its very nature, the substance of the inquiry constitutes a summons to those who think of unity in anything less than the bold christological terms of the New Testament. In this sense it follows the trend which ecumenical thinking has itself taken in the last few years. But it also constitutes a summons to those who draw antinomian deductions from this final unity, and are thus prevented from making the vital contribution which they might be making at the present juncture. Whether or not the detailed arguments are approved or indications followed, response to this twofold summons holds the promise not merely of a deepened and more effective ecumenicity but of real theological and therefore ecclesiastical renewal.

CONTENTS

There is one body, and one Spirit, even as ye are called in one hope of your calling; one Lord, one faith, one baptism, one God and Father of all, who is above all, and through all, and in you all.

— Eph. 4:4-6

CHAPTER ONE

THE SENSE OF UNITY

THROUGHOUT ITS HISTORY the church has always and everywhere maintained an awareness of its unity. It has extended to many different lands and races and cultures. It has taken many different forms. It has been split by innumerable dissensions and disagreements. It has passed through many crises and vicissitudes. It has known ages of the most violent individualism as well as the most submissive collectivism. But for all the legitimate or illegitimate variety it has never lost the sense of its ultimate and indestructible unity.

Sometimes this awareness has found expression in very curious and not particularly Christian forms. It may have led to the attempted creation of a monolithic structure. It may have consisted in a desired compression into distinctive patterns. It may have taken the form of a virtual excommunication of all who seem to threaten the church's unity. But whatever the form of expression, the fact itself is clear. Christians realize that the church ought to be one. Indeed, they know that the final truth about it is unity and not disunity. However circumstances may seem to deny it, the church is one, and cannot cease to reckon with this basic factor.

The ultimate ground of this awareness is the witness of Old and New Testament Scripture. It is not for nothing that in the Old Testament the elect people of God, divided though it was into twelve tribes and later grouped into two kingdoms, consisted of a single race tracing its descent from a single progenitor. It is not for nothing that it was constituted the one nation by redemption out of Egypt, the deliverance at the Red Sea and the giving of the law at Sinai. There might be all kinds of breaches of this unity, from civil war on the one side to foreign marriages on the other. But nothing could shake the final oneness of divine election, redemption, and overruling as focused in the common descent and national membership. The fact that Israel was a national unity clearly meant that it was to be one people.

In the New Testament the national bond is not maintained. The new Israel consists of many peoples, or rather of men gathered out of many peoples. But if the natural grounds of unity are not continued, the various ways in which the church is described make it perfectly clear that we still have to do with a single organism. And the whole structure of the New Testament church or churches shows us that there is a strong and indissoluble sense of unity not only within the local congregation but extending to the church as a whole.

For one thing, the church is still the people of God. Where Gentiles were once "strangers and foreigners," they are now "fellow-citizens with the saints, and of the household of God" (Eph. 2:19). Israel in its older form has been brought to an end. But its end is not its destruction. It is rather its fulfillment. It has emerged as the new Israel, not restricted to one nation, yet still constituting "an holy nation, a peculiar people" (I Pet. 2:9). The external forms of human nationality have been done away. God Himself is King, and the realm to which Christians belong is His kingdom. But the sense of nationhood remains, and with it the awareness of unity.

Again, Christians are described as the temple of God. This can apply to the individual Christian, but it is more generally true of the whole community. All Christians are "builded together [in the Lord] for an habitation of God through the Spirit" (Eph. 2:22). As "lively stones," they are "built up a spiritual house" for the offering up of acceptable spiritual sacrifices (I Pet. 2:5). But the whole lesson of the Old Testament is that there must be only one temple of God. Local shrines can be centers only of an idolatrous worship, even though they may be nominally devoted to the service of God. Hence, if Christians are now to be the temple of God, there cannot be rival houses but only the one and central shrine established upon the one foundation (Eph. 2:20; cf. I Cor. 3:11).

The same lesson is enforced by the comparison of the church with the bride. From the very beginning, marriage has been meant to be monogamous (Gen. 2:24). The deviations of the patriarchs and kings had been exceptions and had normally brought about unhelpful entanglements. The provisions of the law had been concessions to human hardness or weakness. Christ Himself, however, made it quite plain that there can be only the one bride for the one bridegroom (Mark 10:2ff.), and when it is a matter of the Lord Himself as the heavenly Bridegroom there can be no question of polygamy. The bride whom Paul describes in Ephesians 5 can be only one. The marriage between Christ and His people is strictly monogamous. It is right and necessary, therefore, for the church to think of itself as one.

But the fact that the church is called the bride of Christ points us to an even deeper reality of oneness with which it is closely linked. According to the pronouncement of Genesis 2:24, quoted both by our Lord in Matthew 19:5 and Paul in Ephesians 5:31, marriage means that husband and wife become one flesh. If, therefore, Christians are the bride of Christ, this means that the church is one body with Him and the bodies of individual believers are the members of Christ (I Cor. 6:15). In other words, the church is the body of Christ (I Cor. 12:12ff.), or the body of which Christ is the Head (Col. 1:18). But here again, and even more strongly, the lesson of unity is enforced. Within a body there is plenty of scope for diversity. But a man cannot have more than one body. As Christ Himself is one, so the church is necessarily one. Thinking of itself as Christ's body, the church is bound to have an awareness of unity, and to realize that it stands under the obligation to give it practical expression in its life and activity.

The biblical foundation of unity explains the belief in its oneness which the church has been constrained to incorporate in its confession of faith. Believing in Father, Son, and Holy Spirit, Christians must also believe that there is one church. They may be confronted by the phenomenon of disunity. They may feel that their practice falls far short of their profession. They may expose themselves to the cynical gibes of the world. They may experience inward discomfort, disillusion or despair as they say it. But in the light of what they know to be the case, because it belongs to the very essence and foundation of their being, they cannot refuse to confess that there is one church. To do so would be to deny the faith itself. It would be to disbelieve in God. It would be to reject the biblical testimony. It would be to renounce the church and therefore their own being as Christians. In response to the saving work of Christ, in the sight of God and therefore to themselves and to the world, Christians must proclaim their unity, and know that in some way their confession is inalienably true even though the stubborn facts of historical reality may seem to attest the contrary.

On the basis of the biblical witness, and in accordance with the confession, the church necessarily attests its awareness of unity in a constant horror of schism. From the very earliest days, and all through Christian history, there has been the sense that something dreadful and unnatural takes place when professing brethren are either expelled from the church or feel constrained to withdraw for various solid or less solid reasons. We see this already in the primitive church, where excommunication was a solemn sentence to be executed only for the very gravest of offenses. The growth of heresies, and the later schism between East and West, weakened the force of excommunication except in a more restricted context, but there remained a constant sense that those outside the main body could be regarded as Christians only in a very equivocal sense, and an impulse to seek reunification even if necessary by physical as well as spiritual weapons.

How strong was the sense of unity emerged in different ways at the time of the Reformation. Luther felt very keenly his enforced separation from the historic church. Calvin wrote in the strongest terms about the sin of disruption from the visible body, asserting that "no crime can be imagined more atrocious than that of sacrilegiously and perfidiously violating the sacred marriage which the only begotten Son of God has condescended to contract with us" (*Institutes* IV, 1, 10), and explaining carefully that the Reformation is a return to true and catholic unity rather than a flight from it. All the leading Reformers were of the same mind, opposing to the external conformity demanded by traditionalists a true unity of catholic faith and confession.

Indeed, the impulse found practical expression even at this time of disruption. The demand was insistent for a general council, and when it was obvious that the main breach could not be healed, the principle of *cuius regio, eius religio* provided a rough and ready means of preserving at least a territorial or national unity. In face of divergent pressures, this did not always work out in practice. But a substantial measure of local unity remained even though the wider unity of the Western church had been shattered. Even the Anabaptists and Independents, who constituted a serious threat to territorial unity, maintained their own feeling after the unity of the church which they seemed to others so outrageously to violate. For them the individual congregation was the focus of unity, and the principle of the gathered church, together with a strict system of discipline, was designed to secure the unity of the true and pure church as opposed to all external associations.

The tragic increase of denominationalism in the modern world did nothing to destroy this underlying awareness of unity and impulse towards it. Passions might sometimes be roused and sectarian differences magnified. But the intensity of feeling was a paradoxical witness to the realization that there ought to be unity. Even the most exclusivist of churches could always claim that it ardently desired reunification, and even the most fissiparous of sects never imagined that there was an intrinsic value in disunity. It is this basic impulse towards unity, grounded in the Bible and expressed in the confession, which gives the modern ecumenical movement both its justification and appeal even in circles which do not approve its guiding principles or methods. We may not agree what the church is, or what kind of unity it ought to have, or what are the conditions of its attainment, or how it is to be sought, but we all agree that the church ought to be one, and therefore that there ought to be some kind of ecumenical movement in a divided Christendom.

Above all, the sense of unity emerges in the constant prayer for unity with which Christians face the divisive assaults of the old aeon and the actual circumstances of a divided church. That unity should be a subject of petition rests on the dominical precedent of John 17:20ff.: "Neither pray I for these alone, but for them also which shall believe on me through their word; that they all may be one; as thou, Father, art in me, and I in thee, that they also may be one in us; that the world may believe that thou hast sent me. And the glory which thou gavest me I have given them; that they may be one, even as we are one." It is surely significant that some of the most beautiful and earnest of prayers have been for the unity of Christ's people, and that even so disruptive a period as that of the Reformation and its aftermath could give us such petitions as those of the Book of Common Prayer: "Beseeching thee to inspire continually the universal Church with the spirit of truth, unity and concord. And grant, that all they that do confess thy holy Name may agree in the truth of thy holy Word, and live in unity, and godly love." Nor is it the least hopeful sign of modern ecumenicism that, even though conferences may fail and schemes be abandoned, there is a growing volume of prayer that at least in answer to the needs of the world the people of God may find and tread the path of unity.

In the prayer itself Christians may already find their unity. They may not seem to be one in much else, but at least in praying for unity they are brought together. Even more deeply, they are brought into unity with Christ, who was the first to pray that they may be one. This prayer is not an individual or collective caprice. It corresponds to the will of Christ, and therefore to the triumphant reality of God, which lies at the heart of their feeling for unity and gives them the assurance that, notwithstanding all appearances to the contrary, the prayer will find its answer. Prayer for unity is not something which is snatched at as a last resort. It grows out of a deep-seated realization of the truth, and witnesses to it. Nor need it be regarded as a waste of time when the world calls out for bold and constructive action. It has its own objective and subjective power. Above all, it must not be undertaken in a spirit of impotent defiance or resignation. The continuing impulse to pray is itself the work of the indwelling Spirit. And in the knowledge that this is first the prayer of the Son, we may pray it with quiet and obedient confidence in His name, assured that for His sake it is already heard and answered by the Father.

CHAPTER TWO

THE CHALLENGE OF DISUNITY

―――――――

THE CHURCH has an indisputable awareness of its unity. It finds the basis of this in the New Testament concept of the people of God and the New Testament understanding of the Christian community. It has necessarily incorporated it into its confession of faith. It has always tried to give it practical expression even in what seems sometimes to be the crassest of exclusivism or sectarianism. It has rightly made it a topic of urgent and continuing intercession.

Yet against the realization of unity we have to set the stark and discouraging fact of historical disunity. Except perhaps in the very first days of the infant church in Jerusalem, there never has been a time when those who profess and call themselves Christians have in fact lived together in unruffled concord. Even in Jerusalem disputes arose between the Jews and Hellenists (Acts 6:1ff.), and widespread disagreement entered into the primitive churches with the bitter Judaistic controversy (cf. Gal. 1:7ff., 2:1ff.), quite apart from the disruptive influences of incipient Gnosticism.

When we continue the story, we do not find that either the patristic or the medieval period gives us the historical unity that some historians or controversialists would like to imagine. Much of the history of the early church is that of heresies, schisms, and excommunications, with quarrels between the leading churches or bishops to add to the sorry confusion. The Middle Ages give us a more unified picture in the West, but it is overarched by the schism with the Eastern church, not to speak of the Coptic and Syrian. Indeed, even in Europe itself there is the constant discord of warring factions, and doctrinal and religious resistance has often to be suppressed by force to maintain the external facade of unity.

To the continuing schism with the East the Reformation period has added the deep-seated division between Protestantism and Romanism and the sharp antithesis between different kinds of Protestantism. Even among those who hold the basic Christian tenets, there are now scores of churches with distinctive patterns of thought, order, and worship, and in addition there are dogmatic divisions which cut right across the denominational affiliations. Far from presenting a picture of unity to the world, the church seems almost to give a warning example of disunity, the very strength of faith and conviction giving depth and bitterness to the "unhappy divisions." The church may have a consciousness of its unity. But it cannot ignore the stubborn fact of its disunity. And in face of this fact its confession of unity can only seem to be a hollow mockery to itself and especially to the world.

The undeniable reality of disunity confronts us with a question. In view of the fundamental unity of the church, how are we to explain it? What is the reason for this denial by Christians of their true nature? Why is it that God's will for the church seems not to have been realized? To answer this question will not meet the real challenge of disunity. Indeed, it is the easiest part of our task in balancing the unity of the church against its disunity. But at least it will set us on the way to understanding. It will preserve us from idle dreams. It will show us what we are really up against. It will help to close and bolt the door against inadequate concepts of unity, or hopes for its achievement. It is best to begin, therefore, by giving a general answer to this preliminary question.

We must emphasize that only a general answer is possible or necessary in the present context. There are many detailed reasons for particular divisions in the church. The different schisms cannot be fitted into general historical patterns, and to understand them in detail we should have to undertake a complicated historical analysis in each individual case. Yet the fact remains that there are certain overriding considerations which help us to understand the fact of disunity in all its varied manifestations.

The first is the simple and basic truth that the one church of Christ is summoned to live its life and bear its witness in the ordinary circumstances of human life. In this respect a comparison with the individual Christian may be helpful. When a man becomes a Christian he is not removed into a magical sphere where all the problems and tensions of life are removed. Nor is he commanded to try to create such a sphere by artificial withdrawal. If he is a new man in Christ, he has still to be this new man in the old world (I Cor. 5:10) with all its perplexities and entanglements. He can look forward to the coming of Christ when the new order will be set up. He can be confident that his true life is that which is hid with Christ in God (Col. 3:3). But for the moment his job is to be in the world and therefore to face the harsh realities of his environment.

But if this is true of the individual Christian, it is no less true of the church. Having its true nature as the bride and body of Christ, the church in its period of betrothal is left with its great commission in the world (Matt. 28:19, 20), and therefore summoned to give concrete expression to its life as one historical magnitude among others. Even by withdrawal into isolated communities, as attempted both by monastic orders and the sects, it cannot escape its involvement in human affairs. Its present life is a reflection of the incarnation of Christ. It has its real life and nature in its unity with Christ.

But it has necessarily to be the ecclesiastical phenomenon which is all that it often appears to those who belong only to the world. And as such it is ineluctably exposed to the tormenting and disruptive forces and tensions of historical life.

Yet the mere historicity of the church, although it sets us on the way to understanding, is not enough to explain the denial of its inward life. After all, Christ Himself accepted a voluntary exposure to historical forces and circumstances. But He was not involved in inner self-contradiction. He moved through life with a royal superiority to circumstances. He neither withdrew from them on the one side nor did He become their slave on the other. He did not allow the tensions and complexities of life in Roman-occupied Galilee and Judaea to deflect Him from the way of inward righteousness and harmony. The mere fact that life has to be lived in history explains why it may become untrue to itself, but it does not necessarily entail it. Taken direct to heaven, the church would certainly have been safeguarded against the threat of disunity. But why should historical life involve this threat? And why should the church succumb so easily to it?

A preliminary answer which needs to be emphasized is that historical life carries with it a plenitude of legitimate as well as illegitimate diversity. Individuals and races have been richly endowed with a wide range of gifts and tastes and aptitudes. Different men and communities cannot be expected to do everything according to the one strict pattern. It belongs to the very essence of earthly life, and probably of heavenly as well, that there should be many different forms and expressions of the one life. As the Bible itself tells us, there is the one Spirit, but there are diversities of gifts, differences of administrations and diversities of operations (I Cor. 10:4ff.). The only body of Christ has many members with very different tasks and functions (I Cor. 12:12ff.). Hence it is only to be expected that in the historical circumstances of earthly life and according to the good creation of

God there should be varied manifestations of the church and its life.

Diversity, however, is not disunity, and therefore the mere fact of multiplicity is no real answer to the question. But it needs to be emphasized because indirectly it may be a very significant answer. For diversity easily gives rise to disunity, especially when unity itself is confused with uniformity. That is why it is important that this preliminary consideration should be taken into account in tackling the question. Far too often the church has imagined that because it is one it must enforce in the sphere of belief, order, and practice a rigid conformity. But this is neither attainable in practice nor right in principle, and therefore can only lead to revolt and separation in the name of the one Spirit exercising His multiple administration. Disunity itself is not to be easily passed off and excused as legitimate diversity. But the fact that historical life involves multiplicity has been and is a fruitful source of actual disunity when it is not taken into account and there is the impulse to force all individuals, communities, and actions into a narrow and permanent mold. Already in the right and necessary multiplicity of human life we have that which may easily give rise to disunity and even strife in all historical fellowships and institutions and therefore in the church no less than in others.

But the fact that this is so, and that disunity does really arise out of diversity, is due to the third factor which has to be taken into account in this whole question. The life of the church necessarily takes historical form. It is thus involved in multiplicity. But it also falls under the sinfulness which marks all historical life apart from that of the incarnate Christ, and thus involves the constant perversion of unity into uniformity and diversity into disunity. It is because there is no sinless perfection of the church that disunity arises in the community of Jesus Christ for all its awareness and confession of unity.

Here again the comparison with the individual Christian is helpful.   The Christian knows that in Jesus Christ he is called, and called to be, a saint (I Cor. 1:2). He knows that righteousness is of the essence of his new life in Christ. Yet living this life in the varied circumstances of history, he not only knows that he is still guilty of sin, but he realizes that this is so because he still lives in a sinful aeon. Sin runs right through his own life and that of the men around him.   It cannot easily be escaped, whether by withdrawal, suppression, conflict or buoyant confidence. It is one of the things which has to be taken into account on a sober reckoning.   Involvement in a sinful world with its sinful history means sinful failure even for the Christian born from above yet still living here below.

But if this is true of the individual, it is no less true of the whole Christian community. As the bride and body of Christ it has a heavenly calling, and knows and confesses that unity belongs to its true nature. Yet it is not baffled or surprised if it finds that, living and warring in the world, it is guilty of defection from its true nature and implicated in disunity. For it knows that the world in which it lives and works is not only a diverse but also a sinful world. It knows that it is itself composed of sinners. It knows that in so far as it is a historical organization, or complex of organizations, it, too, is sinful. It will not easily acquiesce in its sin. It will be deeply ashamed of its constant denial of its true nature and calling. It will be continually summoned by the Word and Spirit of God to repentance and renewal. It will nerve itself in the Lord to resistance and reformation and conquest. But it will have no illusions as to the difficulty of its task, and therefore it will not be disillusioned at its many and serious failures. The very fact that it is in history means that it is in sinful history, and therefore liable to slide from legitimate diversity into illegitimate disunity, or to confound genuine unity with artificial and aggravating uniformity.

The fact of disunity need not, then, be evaded or minimized or explained away. For a church of sinners, belonging to the kingdom of heaven but wayfaring and warring in the kingdom of this world, there is a dialectical tension between what it is by its new and true nature and what it still is in the continuing fact of its old and past nature. The tension is not merely between the heavenly and the earthly, the spiritual and the physical.   Jesus Christ Himself lived a genuine earthly life, though He was also the Lord from heaven (I Cor. 15:47). He lived in the body. And yet He was free from this tension. The tension is between the new aeon and the old, the man in Christ and the man of sin, the heavenly nature and the sinful historical nature (Eph. 4:17ff.). In the light of this being of the church as a colony of heaven on earth (Phil. 3:20), and therefore subject to earthly pressures, it is easy enough to see why disunity and other defections should seem to give the lie to its genuine nature.

But if the explanation is easy, it is not so easy to answer the deeper question and challenge implicit in the church's disunity. The church senses and confesses its unity. It is confronted by the incontestable fact of its disunity. Does this mean, then, that the protested unity is not as genuine a reality, or a reality of the same order, as the flagrant and undeniable disunity? Surely not even the church or a Christian can be both united and divided at one and the same time. Surely the one reality must yield to the other, or be content with a restricted kingdom where it may establish itself and rule with unassailable majesty. Surely a dual allegiance is not possible unless the one authority is subject to the other, or there is a partition in which each is given its proper sphere of influence.

It is this deeper question which constitutes the true problem of disunity. The fact is clear enough. The explanation of the fact offers no great difficulty. But to reconcile the fact with the contradictory fact of unity is a serious problem, not only in itself but more penetratingly in its relationship to the saving work of God which forms the sum and substance of the gospel and the Christian faith. False solutions to this problem constitute a threat both to the historical life and witness of the church and to the work of Christ, or rather to the understanding of the work of Christ, which underlies them. It is to this basic problem that we must now turn; and we must first explore and seal off the two main blind alleys into which the church has been betrayed in its attempts to find a solution.

CHAPTER THREE

ORGANIZATIONAL UNITY

THE CHURCH cannot, of course, deny its unity even in face of undeniable disunity. It must find some solution to the problem of contradiction. And the bold and simple way is surely to meet the fact of disunity head-on, to force it to give ground, to resist the forces of division and disintegration on their own ground, to impose a historical unity in focus upon an accepted center, to demonstrate the superiority of the fact of unity over the threat of disunity. In other words, unity must be achieved and asserted at all costs as a demonstrable historical entity, and everything that will not or cannot fit into this pattern must be rejected as the church, or allowed as such only as it were *per nefas* and on the left hand.

Consciously or unconsciously this way has often been taken in the thought and action of the church, as we have noted already in our reference to the impulse towards unity. It may take many forms according to the different views of the accepted center and the nature of the organization. Indeed, even in the one historical grouping the actual forms may vary from age to age. They may be more restricted in the one case and more generous in the other. But for all the differences and even contradictions they are one in principle, sharing the same strength but also vitiated by the same errors. A brief description of some of the leading forms will help us to understand the type of solution attempted.

The most obvious and outstanding example is the association of churches grouped from a very early time under the bishop of Rome and today constituting the largest numerical body of professing Christians in the world. The feature of this communion is not, of course, a rigid uniformity in doctrine or belief, for Rome has been wise enough in the course of its history to allow for considerable wealth and diversity in the expression of Christian life. What characterizes it is a common body of defined and essential dogma, a common discipline, and the ultimate focus of a common allegiance to the pope as the successor of Peter and the vicar of Christ. That which accepts this allegiance is the catholic church, and is therefore one. That which does not may in a sense be Christian, but only equivocally and doubtfully. In any case, however, the problem of disunity is not so much a problem for the church itself with its unbroken unity. It is a problem for those who have separated themselves from the church, yet still wish to belong to it.

Another form, hardly less sharply defined but less intransigent, is that asserted by many Anglicans. The catholic church is the inter-communicating company of those who have preserved the Bible, the early creeds, the two sacraments, and the historic ministry. In this case there may be a wide variety in practice and teaching, and no closely knit organization is required. But historical entities are made the focus of a clearly definable and attainable unity. Where these are present, there is the catholic church and it is demonstrably one. Where they are not present, or not fully present, the most that can be said is that we have associations of Christians which can be described as churches or the church only in a defective or charitable sense. And again the problem of disunity is that of those who have willfully or otherwise abandoned the historic guarantees and centers of unity.

The state church might almost be described as a variant of the same notion. In this case, of course, there is no claim to be the one catholic church or an association of catholic

churches.   A geographical or historical construct is almost
shamelessly taken as the focus of unity.   The church in any
one state is the national church, recognizing similar churches
outside its borders but constituting a single organized unit in
the one political entity.   Now it is evident that for practical
purposes even the Roman and Anglican and any other views
of attainable organizational unity have to take into account
the groupings of history.   Indeed, even in the New Testament itself the one church found local expression in the
churches of different cities or provinces.   But now the state
church is itself in this particular place the visibly united
catholic church, and the only problem of disunity is that of
schismatics and nonconformists who try to be Christians
outside the church of their own state.

But the separatist understanding of the church provides
us with yet another version.   In some circles it is far too
easily assumed that schismatics contented themselves with an
invisible unity and had no concern for the visible.   The very
opposite is really the case.   In true independency the congregation might be taken as the only focus of unity.   But the
whole point is that in the congregation we have a gathered
body of believers, united in many cases by a covenant, accepting a common code of belief and conduct, and exercising
a strict internal discipline.   The attempt is thus made to
achieve and maintain a visible unity at the local level by
restriction of entry, enforcement of a standard, and strict
exclusion of those guilty of doctrinal or practical deviation.
The congregation is the church; and whereas individual
Christians outside it might belong to the mystical body of
Christ, so-called churches or Christian associations apart
from or out of communion with the congregation cannot be
regarded as the church in any true or strict sense.   In a
different form and at a different level the same exclusivism
rules as in the Roman Catholic church, and unity can be
asserted in virtue of exclusion according to a fixed historical
norm.

Finally, there is at least a tendency to think that unity may be attained in the form of a confederation of churches under some such body as the World Council of Churches. It would be too much to say that any or many of those associated with this movement would argue that the catholic church either is or will be the aggregate of constituent members. But with the promotion and accomplishment of schemes of union, and the development of the World Council and its organization, there is the very real danger in practice of membership coming to be equated in some sense with this new historical norm. Already there is the tendency in some quarters to advance the claim that if the voice of the church is to be known, or the work of the church to be done, or this or that arrangement with a secular authority to be made, the only regular channel is through the World Council, as though this were really the church and non-associated bodies were merely sects. The dogmatic thinking of the ecumenical movement is fortunately tending in a very different direction. We may thus hope that the practical assumption will never find doctrinal formulation but undergo the necessary theological correction. In effect, however, such a body as the World Council does offer an alternative and attractive route of historical realization of unity in accordance with its simple and not too exacting standard of membership.

Now it must be clearly recognized that this attempted actualization of unity in historical terms has many commendable features. In the first place, it derives from a right impulse in the knowledge that the church is and ought to be one. There would be something amiss if Christians allowed their sense of unity to fade in face of the obvious fact of disunity. The awareness of unity rightly and necessarily impels to ventures of this nature. They may take extravagant and unwholesome forms. They may give rein to the worst excesses of human pride, arrogance, censoriousness, and even cruelty. But in underlying impulse they cannot be dismissed as perverted or unnecessary.

Again, the attempt at historical actualization is surely commendable in spirit. The Christian is to preserve a proper meekness and humility. At the right point and in the right way he is not to resist evil (Matt. 5:39). But he is called to be a fighter against wrong in himself (Gal. 5:14). And if this is true of the individual Christian, it is true of the community. Disunity may be a fact. But it is not a fact to be tamely accepted and deplored. It is a fact to be resisted. It is a fact to be vanquished. Even though it be a hydra-headed monster, even though the final overthrow of this fact may not be possible in this time of warfare and pilgrimage, there must be no surrender. To be sure, fighting involves hardship, discipline, and even a certain ruthlessness. In the course of the struggle friends may be hurt as well as foes. The campaign as a whole may in some cases serve the wrong cause better than the right. But the active spirit of resistance deserves our commendation.

Third, it is right in its appreciation that unity must be given practical shape. True Christianity knows nothing of a divorce between the spiritual and the historical. The mystical unity is unreal if it does not find expression in at least an attempt at historical unity. The church cannot be content to be one in faith and spirit and possibly charity if it is hopelessly divided in organization and practical endeavor. It is committed by its very being in history to give a concrete, historical representation of what it is in terms of the historical life which the world can see and understand. This is plainly grasped in the various efforts to achieve and maintain unity as a demonstrable historical entity.

Fourth, it is right in the sense that it points to certain elements or patterns which must have a place in the united church, and will indeed serve as helpful means to true reunification. We shall have to return to these in detail at a later stage. But for the moment it may be noted that the feelings after historical centers of unity have not been wholly misguided or futile. Much is to be learned from the various attempts made, and the actual attack upon disunity will necessarily follow the lines suggested.

In view of these commendable features, it may be admitted that the way of historical realization has many of the characteristics of the path of true unity in face of disunity. Yet it is a blind alley just the same. And it is so in the first instance for the very simple reason that it does not achieve its goal. It contributes no less and perhaps even more to disunity than it does to unity. The true church can be one only by the rigorous process of excluding many others who also call themselves Christians and are perhaps convinced that in their own organization they, too, are the true church. The one church expels or alienates or contests with a multitude of warring sects, and by its very attempt at the achievement and assertion of unity adds to the bitterness and disruption. In the head-on clash, it is disunity which always emerges the victor.

Again, it is a way which cannot consistently be pursued. The Romanist church may excommunicate heretics, but if they are willing to confess that Jesus Christ is Savior and Lord it cannot presume to say that they are not Christians, and therefore exclude them in every sense from the church. The Reformers may describe the medieval church as a synagogue of Satan and a false church, but they cannot strictly refuse it the character of a real church, or claim that there are not true congregations or Christians within it. The modern Roman church may claim that it alone is the catholic church, yet it cannot draw what seems to be the logical deduction and unchurch all others. Anglo-catholics may argue that bishops are of the *esse* of the church, yet the church obstinately remains even where there are no bishops. The strictest of sects may reduce itself and therefore the pure church to a tiny handful, yet recourse must always be had to a larger mystical body in which at least a few others can find a place. An ecumenical confederation of churches may act as though it were the church, yet it knows perfectly well that those who for good or less good reasons stay outside cannot be treated as though they were not Christians or Christian churches. In other words, the church cannot in fact be equated with the more or less perfectly achieved historical entity.

Thirdly, and more deeply, it makes the mistake of finding its practical focus or center of unity in a historical factor, as though the church were only or primarily a human entity like so many others. To be sure, lip service is always paid to the more basic center in Jesus Christ, and His atoning work, and faith in Him, and the action of the Holy Spirit. But where the challenge of disunity is met in these terms, these basic realities are not taken with sufficient seriousness or given the place which they ought to occupy in the considering and answering of this whole question. To put it in the familiar terms of the doctrine of justification, what we have here is always in some sense and to some degree the attempt at a unity of works. As such it is praiseworthy in impulse, in spirit, and in the realization that there have to be works. Indeed, it may at times achieve some imposing results just as the effort at self-justification can present us with outstanding examples of the religious life. But since it does not begin at the right place, and is not orientated to the true center or enabled by the right power, it cannot and will not achieve a proper or durable result.

The underlying fault is not to take Christ Himself as the real starting-point and center. But this failure carries with it a radical failure in understanding as well as procedure and power. The incarnational pattern of the church's unity is not perceived. It is rightly emphasized that it must take flesh. But the no less necessary emphasis is not so clear that it is twofold in nature. In Eutychian fashion, the divine-human and human unity are so closely equated that the unity of the ecclesiastical institution or association is regarded directly as that of the church. This may lead to the investing of the institution with a false divinity. But it may equally well avenge itself by a swallowing up of the inward unity in the outward, so that there can be little or no perception of the ultimate unity of the church in Christ. Either way there is a confusion of the divine-human and human natures in which the former cannot be seen in its true importance or exercise its living force. And the final result is a unified and to some extent ossified human construct not very obviously distinguishable from similar constructs and certainly quite unable to secure or guarantee the unity which it professes to embody. Missing its incarnational duality, the church claims too much, and therefore at root too little. It is finally for this reason that its powerful and intrinsically justifiable assertion of historical unity does not and cannot constitute any real answer to the challenge of disunity, and the end of the blind alley can be only a fanatical exclusivism which ignores the facts, a liberalizing relativization which seeks a compromise, or a weary disillusionment which either abandons the whole enterprise or seeks a very different and equally unsatisfactory solution.

CHAPTER FOUR

INVISIBLE UNITY

IN CONTRAST TO those who meet the challenge of disunity head-on, there are others who try to save the unity of the church by tactics of evasion or compromise. They recognize that disunity is an incontestable fact. They see that historical unity is not to be expected in any substantial or satisfactory measure. They cannot accept what they know to be untrue, namely, that the church is not one. And so they take refuge in a sphere where historical disunity cannot enter. In place of organizational disunity, and side by side with regrettable but accepted division, they believe and maintain an invisible unity of the church.

Up to a point, this is a way which almost all Christians have taken in some form. Indeed, the fact that they have often done so even when attempting to create an inflexible historical unity testifies to the recognition that the unity of the church is something deeper and more enduring than that of a historical construct. And it is always comforting, of course, to have an inviolable sanctuary of mystical unity to which to escape when our material unities fail to stand up to the critical scrutiny of fact.

The way in which invisible unity is asserted may vary considerably. In some cases, it is rightly sought in Christ, though more particularly in Christ ascended and seated at the right hand of the Father. Sometimes it is characterized as spiritual, not so much in the older sense of unity in the Holy Spirit, but in the more modern and questionable sense of spiritual as opposed to material. Sometimes it takes an emotional form. It is the experienced unity of Christians as they live the Christian life or meet for edification or combine in Christian enterprise. Sometimes it is platonized as an ideal of unity which the church has never attained but by which it is to shape its conduct and towards which it must always strive. Sometimes it is not given any very precise sense and does not convey any particular notion, but is simply a vague, mystical unity to which appeal can be made when no other answer can be seen to the pressing challenge of disunity.

Now we must not conclude too hastily that the assertion of an invisible unity is wrong even in these inadequate forms. In this second blind alley, too, there are features which we shall find again on the right way; and as we explore this second *cul-de-sac* (or is it really an attempted short-cut?) it is as well that we should begin by learning from it what is to be learned.

In the first place, it gives us a more realistic appraisal of the fact of disunity than that of the opposite extreme. It does not minimize the threat presented. It sees the inadequacy of purely human defenses. It is not necessarily guilty of a cowardly resignation, but rather of courageous honesty, when it withdraws upon an inner and impregnable citadel. If its realism is not really great enough, at least it compares favorably with the obstinate blindness to realities which impels many Christians to force through an organizational unity.

Second, it recognizes that the unity of the church must be the work of God and not of man. As we shall see, it is perhaps deficient in its estimate of the work of God. But at least it sees that it is God's work. It is for this reason that it finds it in a sphere of transcendence where the divisions of the present order cannot obtain. It cannot think that as God's work the unity of the church can be such a botched and precarious business as appears in church history. It is jealous for the honor of God and the perfection and certainty of His work. And it finds in the perfect invisible unity of the church a transcendent and superior work against which the facts of disunity dash themselves in vain.

Third, and along the same lines, it has a perception of the fact that there is a contrast between the temporal and the eternal, and that it is the eternal which really counts (I Cor. 4:18). In this respect it bears an important witness to a materialistic age like our own which so easily concludes that the only true facts are those of measurable phenomena. To assert the invisible unity of the church is not necessarily, or at any rate consciously, to be guilty of a flight from reality. It is to undertake a flight to the true reality. It is to see things in their proper perspective. If there is error in the way in which this is often done, there is also truth in the fact that it is attempted.

Fourth, there can be no doubt that behind the fellowship which Christians do know even across denominational as well as geographical, economic, political, and social frontiers, we have to recognize a genuine work of the Holy Spirit. The fact that in its human form this may be emotional does not mean that it is unreal, or not of God. It may fall short of what the Holy Spirit intends. So do all our expressions of unity. But it is not an imaginary substitute for genuine unity in the Spirit. To decry this unity, or to deal harshly or impatiently with those who think that it is perhaps enough, may well be to quench the work of the Holy Ghost rather than to advance it.

Fifth, and finally, there is a true biblical sense in which the unity of the church, and the whole life of Christians and the Christian community, is invisible during this time between Christ's ascension and return. After all, does not Paul tell us that we walk by faith and not by sight (II Cor. 5:7)? Is it not of the essence of faith to be the evidence of things not seen (Heb. 11:1)? Are not the true and enduring realities those which are not seen (II Cor. 4:18)? Is not our real life hid with Christ in God (Col. 3:3)? Do we really see ourselves as righteous, or saints, or a kingdom of priests? Do we not try to evade the demand and discipline of faith if we will not accept the given unity of the church unless we can have a visible demonstration? Is not the whole point of a unity of faith as opposed to that of works the fact that it is accepted as created and given by God, and therefore believed even though it seems to be contradicted by the realities of this sinful order? In this respect and along these lines the doctrine of the invisible church carries with it a valuable and scriptural insight to which due weight must be given in our estimate of this whole question.

On the other hand, there are dangers in this whole approach which justify us describing it as a blind alley in the form in which it is usually found. We may begin, perhaps, with the obvious weakness that it leaves disunity in triumphant possession of a whole area of the church's life. Indeed, the disunity may often be excused as an expression of legitimate diversity. If not, it can be shrugged off as finally unimportant though necessary in the regrettable circumstances of the present order. But conflict with it is avoided, because the unity and the disunity operate on different levels. In this world, therefore, disunity remains the dominant and triumphant factor.

This leads us to the second criticism that if the way of organizational unity is one of attempted self-righteousness this is far too easily one of culpable antinomianism. It rejoices in the assured fact of invisible unity. But its faith does not lead, as faith should, to vigorous and obedient action. It is a resigned and passive faith. To be sure, faith is primarily receptive. It is not itself a work of justifying righteousness. But on a genuine biblical and Reformation view faith is also active. It is a busy, vital, inspiring, and impelling force. It must express that which it believes in terms of human life and activity. It must engage the forces of evil which it knows to be defeated. It cannot acquiesce in the disunity which it knows not to be the real truth about the church. It may fail in its attempted expression of unity. It knows that the full reality of unity is to be found in that which God has done. But just because this is known in faith to be the real truth, faith is impelled to give it preliminary and fragmentary expression. Otherwise it is surely not a true faith.

The question thus poses itself whether we really do believe in the invisible unity of the church if we are not prepared, as Calvin and Cranmer were, to seek its visible concretion in every area of church life and to the very utmost of our power. After all, the justified sinner may be still a sinner. But he cannot be an acquiescent sinner, abandoning this life to the triumphant fact of sin, because he can appeal in another and higher sphere to the even more triumphant fact of righteousness. And by the same token, the united church may be still disunited, but it cannot be acquiescently disunited, abandoning this life to triumphant disunity because it can appeal in a different sphere to a higher and ultimate unity. To the extent that it is so often antinomian, the appeal to an invisible unity can only be described as a *cul-de-sac* or attempted short cut.

But it is not always antinomian. For where it is thought of as an ideal unity, it may sometimes be regarded as an inspiration to unity. And what is minimized or misunderstood is the given fact of a unity already achieved. Or again, a genuine historical concretion is perceived, but it is restricted to a particular psychical or emotional or spiritual area of life and need not, or perhaps cannot, be translated into practical terms. To these variants the first two criticisms do not apply, or are only partially applicable. We have thus to ask whether there is a deeper and more comprehensive reason why we cannot take any variant of this way.

The answer is twofold. In the first place, the way involves in all its forms a measure of dualism which vitiates its whole understanding. The dualism may be between the heavenly and the earthly, the ideal and the real, or the spiritual and the physical. But at some point a solution is always found in separation. Unity belongs to the one sphere, but not to the other. To the extent that the view is informed or corrected by genuinely biblical teaching, the separation is not always so clear or fatal as in genuine dualism. But it cannot easily be denied that a dualistic separation dominates or pervades this whole answer. And it is on this basis and for this reason that it so often degenerates into an antinomian escape. On the one side of the fence there is a harsh world in which unity is difficult or impossible; on the other a very different world in which it is assured and easy. What more obvious, then, than to escape either mentally or practically from the harsh and difficult into the easy and comfortable? The fact that there is a very definite opposition between the old aeon and the new gives an air of plausibility to the whole construction even when it takes the more blatantly gnostic form of a dualism of the spiritual and corporal. But the fact remains that a wrong line of demarcation is drawn, with fatal consequences for the understanding of unity and disunity.

But this leads us at once to the second point, and the final criticism of this whole way, namely, that it entails like the first blind alley a basic overlooking of Christ and therefore a perversion of the incarnational pattern of the church's unity. Christ is seen, of course; but there is a short cut to Christ in heaven, and a minimizing of the fact that it is the Incarnate who is now the Resurrected and Ascended. In consequence, the church itself is understood with a constant tendency to Docetism or at very best Nestorianism. The church is one in its divine-human nature. But this united church never assumes more than the semblance of a church in the world of historical reality. Or it is accompanied by a human construct or complex which is fragmentary and human, and cannot be brought into any strict relationship with the true and unified reality of the church in heaven.

Either way, the church thinks and acts as though in its final reality it could already live the life of heaven, and historical existence were only an improper or unrelated life to be endured with all its contradictions, ignominies, and failures, or at most to be pursued in relative independence of the true reality.   In its Nestorian impulses this way can easily lead by reversion to what seems to be its direct opposite, just as its Docetism may finally issue in a renewed Eutychianism, and Eutychianism to Docetism and Nestorianism.   But in general tendency the incarnational duality is now overemphasized to the point of dualism, or the separation of a sphere of reality from a sphere of semblance.   The church now claims too little, and therefore in the last analysis too much.   It is for this reason that the powerful and intrinsically justifiable assertion of an invisible unity is not enough in answer to the challenge of disunity, and the end of this blind alley can only be an antinomianism which refuses its proper task, an escapism which flees reality, or a repressed but irrespressible activism which finally revolts against the reality of an invisible or ideal unity and impetuously rushes from one *cul-de-sac* to another.

CHAPTER FIVE

UNITY IN CHRIST

As WE HAVE SEEN, the insistence upon organizational unity on the one side, or invisible unity on the other, does not give us an adequate answer to the challenge of disunity. On both sides there are valuable elements of truth which must have a place in a true answer. But neither of itself is sufficient in practice; and while the two may just as well be complementary as contradictory they do not easily combine in a satisfactory and invincible partnership.

Are we to conclude, then, that the final word rests with disunity? Is the enforced unity, the escape to a sphere of invisibility, or some form of uneasy compromise between them, the best that can be done in impossible circumstances? A realistic appraisal of the situation shows us that there is a sense in which we cannot hope to destroy the threat and challenge of disunity so long as the church remains in this world. In this sphere, too, it must always be the church militant. Yet this does not mean that it must be a defeated or despairing church. It must be a church which knows that the power of unity is greater than that of disunity; that for all the discouragements and setbacks and assaults the victory is already won; that it is not the helpless victim but the master of circumstances. But how can it know this when even its best efforts seem to lead only to the greater disruption?

We can see the answer to this question when we appreciate the underlying reason for the inadequacy of attempted assertions of unity. In different ways and at different points and to different degrees those who aim at organizational or invisible unity do not really take seriously the fact that first and last and all the time they must seek and find their unity in Christ Himself, and therefore in God. It is because of this prior failure that their best efforts and aspirations are also foredoomed to failure. And it is when this prior defect is remedied that there can be hope of a successful meeting of the challenge of disunity.

It must be recognized, of course, that Christ is not completely ignored in the methods suggested. Those who find unity in the church or certain of its institutions usually emphasize that Christ Himself has founded the church and its institutions, so that in the last resort they unify in virtue of His divine appointment as Lord and Master. Again, those who look beyond the disunities of the present order to a mystical unity do not think in exclusively platonic or gnostic terms, but find this unity in the ascended Son. Is it not an exaggeration, therefore, to blame their failure on a basic failure to find an impregnable and victorious and impelling unity in Christ?

There are two answers to this question: first, that they do not take seriously enough the fact that Christ Himself really is the unity of the church; and second, that with conflicting but equally erroneous over-emphases they misunderstand the way in which this is the case. The second point will demand fuller attention in Chapter 7, but since it obviously overlaps the first we may say already that it is not enough either to find the focus of unity in an institution founded by Christ or to find it in a heavenly order of salvation inaugurated by Him. To do this is to fail to find in Jesus Christ Himself, incarnate and crucified as well as resurrected and ascended, the true basis and center of the church's unity, its full and indestructible actualization, and therefore the one secure and triumphant answer to the false, if very real, assaults of disunity.

The fact is that Christ Himself in His person and work is already the accomplished unity of the church. It is because of this that the church knows that it is already one, and can work and pray for the visible manifestation of its unity. If it is the one people, this is not merely because it is a people; it is because it is the people of which Christ is the one King. If it is the one temple, this is not merely because it is a single if diverse and rambling structure; it is because it is indwelt by the one God. If it is the one bride, this is not in virtue of its unity as an individual entity, but in virtue of its betrothal to the one Bridegroom. If it is the one body, this is not because the church itself is of itself an organism, but because it is the body of Christ, and He Himself is one. The basis, focus, center, and substance of the church's unity is Christ Himself as its Savior, Lord, and Head.

But what do we mean when we say this? After all, Christians have always realized and confessed that they are ultimately united in the one Christ. Yet this does not seem to have given them any greater power against disunity, or to have exercised any very powerful effect on their thinking and action. In what respect, therefore, is it necessary to go to Christ afresh for a sure and convincing answer to our present problem?

First, it is a matter of emphasis. In the thinking and action of too many Christians, in this as in so many other matters of doctrine and practice, Christ is assumed as a kind of background reality. But if Christ is really the Lord and Head and Savior of the church He cannot be assumed in the background. He cannot be expected to work indirectly. He cannot be allowed to operate only in subjection to lesser media or in a restricted sphere. He Himself must always stand in the foreground. Through every medium and in every sphere it must be He Himself who is at work. The emphasis must always fall primarily and decisively upon Him. Otherwise He is not taken seriously as the true basis and center, and all kinds of unnecessary deviations and dif-

ficulties will arise in the detailed thinking and outworking.
If Christ is accepted as the underlying and ultimate basis of
unity, then the implications of this fact must be grasped,
and the fact itself must dominate all discussion and action.
It is because, even on this accepted basis, those rejected
means of unity are really looking to other centers, in fact
if not in intention, that they fail to give us the necessary
answer, for all the guidance that they offer once we learn
consciously and emphatically to put Christ in the center.

Second, it is a matter of understanding. When we say that
the basis and center of unity are to be found in Christ, we
do not mean only that He is a unifying factor, i.e., that we
are all united because we believe in Him, and profess to
follow Him, and hope to live and reign with Him. For at
root this usually means that the unity is still to be found
in us, namely, in our common faith and discipleship and
hope. What is meant is quite strictly that Jesus Christ is the
unity of His people. He is not merely the focus of unity.
He is also its substance. The unity of the church is already
an accomplished fact in Christ.

Interpreted in the light of the New, the Old Testament
gives us valuable light on this truth. It is of the very essence
of Israel that it derives from the one progenitor, so that ultimately its unity does not consist in its common speech or
land or history or institutions but in Abraham himself as its
father. Again, it is of the very essence of the temple that
it points forward to the one individual in whose body the
Word is to take flesh and dwell among us (John 1:14).
Again, it is of the very essence of Eve as the first bride
that she is bone of Adam's bone and flesh of his flesh, so
that she has her very life in him (Gen. 2:23). These different pictures all lead up to the tremendous truth that the one
Christ is the very life of His people, and therefore their wisdom, righteousness, sanctification, and unity (I Cor. 1:30).

The difficulty which the church has always experienced
with this truth is twofold. In the first place, it does not see

its total range and depth. In pride, self-will, or ignorance it will not allow that Christ is now its only and total life. It will not permit Him to be what He came to be and really is, namely, its Representative and Substitute, the One who has taken its place, doing for it and being for it what it cannot do and be for itself. But this is where we must begin if we are genuinely to see Christ as our unity, and to know the power and victory of unity against disunity. In this as in every other sphere we must see and accept the humbling but saving and exalting fact that where we fail and sin and separate, Christ Himself has come in our place, setting us aside to act for us and to regather us in Him. We do not and cannot find our unity in Christ unless we are prepared to find it in Him, not merely as the Founder of Christianity or the Focus of a spiritual fellowship, but as our incarnate, crucified and ascended Substitute.

In the second place, however, it finds it hard to accept it as a real fact. The two difficulties are obviously related. There can be no doubt as to the unity of Christ Himself. This is a self-evident fact. But unless we see that Christ is really our Representative, that the church exists only as its life is in Him, we cannot see so easily that the unity of the church is also a real fact in Him. It is so much easier to speak as if disunity were the real truth. It demands so much less faith to regard the unity in Christ as merely a starting-point, or an ideal, or a mystical unity remote from and comfortably superior to the harsh actualities of life. Even if Christ is verbally accepted as Substitute, it is so much more human to speak and act as if unity, like righteousness and wisdom and sanctification, were merely a judicial pronouncement, as though the Word of God were not at once His act, and what God pronounces were not the new and true reality before which the old and false must yield and perish.

Yet the whole point of the gospel is that God no longer deals with man as he is in himself. Now that Christ has come as the representative man, taking the place of all others, God deals with the human race in Him. What is found in historical and sinful life is still a real fact. But it is a defeated and perishing fact. It has been taken to the cross and judged and done away in the Sin-bearer. It has been replaced by the new and true fact of the life of Jesus Christ incarnate and resurrected (cf. II Cor. 5:14). The genuine reality of man, i.e., his reality as seen by God, and therefore his true and future and eternal reality, is that of the being into which he has already entered in virtue of the substitutionary work of Christ, and which he may already know by faith in Him. God Himself has acted for man to meet the challenge of disunity. In the one Christ taking the place of all others He has given the convincing and triumphant answer of unity: "All one in Christ Jesus" (Gal. 3:28).

This unity in Christ is an invincible unity in face of human disunity because it has been accomplished for us by the act of God Himself. Faith is thus right, and truly realistic, to believe it as something superior even though not yet seen and apparently contradicted by the realities of human life. But it must not believe it merely as a declaration, or a kind of legal sentence, or a future hope, or an overarching ideal. It must believe it as a real fact already worked out for us representatively in the life and death and resurrection of Jesus Christ. It must be the higher realism which sees the divine and therefore the true and final fact triumphantly opposed to every human opposition.

It is when unity in Christ is seen and accepted as a real fact that we can have the quiet assurance in face of disunity that no attempt at purely human unification can ever give. In Christ the will of God is already done; His kingdom has come; the prayer for unity is heard and answered. All further action can proceed upon this given fact, not in an evasion of reality, but in a recognition of the true reality. Not to believe this, and therefore to think that some other unity must be found or created, is to live as though the incarnation, death, and resurrection of Christ had not taken place or had not taken place for us, and can therefore only lead to the greater disunity. To believe it, and therefore to be content to find our unity achieved and given as a real fact in Christ, is to find the solid and enduring answer to the challenge of disunity, and therefore to set ourselves on the way to the defeat of its damaging and despairing if impotent counter-thrusts.

For when unity in Christ is seen and accepted as a real fact, our quiet assurance is also an impulsion to action. Unity no less than wisdom and sanctification is our true being. It cannot remain an unexpressed reality. It demands outworking in the complementary action of those who are willing to see their independent reality judged and set aside, and to find their new and true reality in the One who took their place. This action itself cannot be independent. It must find its origin and power and goal wholly and continually in Christ. Otherwise it can only lead again to fresh division, to the disintegration which is the inevitable lot of sinful life and action outside of Christ. But it really is an action. It is the living out of the life in Christ. And therefore it must and will find its provisional but very real expression in genuine unification, thus attesting to the world and to itself that it has found in Christ a superior and compelling unity.

The church is one church, whatever the facts may seem to say, because Christ is one, and because He is one for the church, and because the only true life of the church is that which it has in Him. This is our sole but sole-sufficient answer to the problem of disunity in a sinful order. This is the solid basis of our confession of unity, and the starting-point for all our attempts at its practical expression. The unity of the church exists already and indestructibly in Jesus Christ. It *is* one in Him.

CHAPTER SIX

UNITY IN THE FATHER
AND THE SPIRIT

———

JESUS CHRIST, however, is not alone. His action as our Representative and Substitute is that of the Trinity. Father and Spirit are no less active than the Son in the accomplishment of our salvation. The unity which we have in Christ is thus a unity in the Father and in the Holy Spirit. And before we consider in greater detail what it means that we are united in Christ, it will be helpful to pause for a moment in order that we may grasp this wider implication.

The fact that Christians are united in the Father is plainly suggested in the prayer of Jesus in John 17:21: "As thou, Father, art in me, and I in thee, that they also may be one in us." It follows from the fact that Jesus does not act alone when He takes the place of sinners and brings in their new life. He acts as the Elect of God and the Only-begotten of the Father. To be united with Christ is thus to be united with the One who is Himself in a relationship of distinctive and enduring unity with the Father and therefore to be caught up in relationship of unity with Him, and in Him with one another.

It is here that we see particularly the bearing of the fact that the church is the one people of God. To be sure, this is because it derives from the one Head, namely, Jesus Christ. But deriving from this Head it is the people of the one God. For this Head from whom it derives and in whom it has its life is the Elect of God. He is indeed the Elect of God from all eternity. But He is the Elect in history too. He is the Elect in whom there is summed up the prophetic history of Old Testament Israel from whom He springs. He is the Elect for us, fulfilling the covenant which otherwise could only be broken on our side, and thus making possible our election in Him, and therefore our constitution as the covenant people. To be in Christ is to be a member of the people to whom God says: "I will be your God, and ye shall be my people" (Jer. 11:4). It is therefore to be united, not merely by a common membership of this people, but by the common election of the one God. Elect in Christ, we have the one electing Father as our God and therefore we are one people in Him.

There is, of course, no opposition between unity in Christ and unity in the Father. It has been the mistake of many doctrines of election and the covenant to drive a wedge at this point, as though there were two foci of unity. But Christ Himself warns us that this is not the case. If we are one in the Father and the Son, it is because they themselves are one: "Thou in me, and I in thee" (John 17:21). We are elect and well pleasing to God only as Christ is well pleasing (Mark 1:11) and the Elect for us. We are the people of the covenant only as we are the people of Christ who has fulfilled the covenant for us. But because this is the case, because He really has fulfilled the covenant, and is the Elect of God, well pleasing to His Father both in time and from all eternity, we are genuinely the people of God, and therefore the one people of the one God in the one Christ.

But there is an even deeper truth to be seen at this point. For the people of God descend from a single progenitor, and are therefore not merely a nation but a family. Now in a sense it is true that Christ is the Head and therefore the Progenitor of His people. It is from Him that we derive our life, and in Him that we have it. But Christ Himself is the Son of the Father. To be in Him is to be in the Son.

It is thus to have a share in His Sonship. It is to be able to say: "Our Father" (Matt. 6:9). It is to receive the adoption of sons, "whereby we cry, Abba, Father" (Rom. 8:15). It is "to be conformed to the image of his Son, that he might be the firstborn among many brethren." It is to belong to the family of God, and therefore to have not only the one Lord, but also, and in Him, "the one God and Father of all, who is above all, and through all, and in you all" (Eph. 4:6). It is to have the one life of the one family, and therefore to be indestructibly united in the one relationship.

Here again, of course, there must be no question of finding a brotherhood under the divine Father apart from the Son. This can only lead into the sphere of idealistic make-believe, and finally entail the serious disillusionment which leaves disunity the more triumphant. We are not the children of this Father by nature, but only by adoption (Rom. 8:15). And as we are elect and well pleasing only in Jesus Christ, we are adopted only in Jesus Christ. We cannot be autonomous Christs. We are not the children of God in our own right. Indeed, we can never be sons of God as Jesus Christ is. But in Him, the Only-begotten, we really can be sons, i.e., to the extent that in His incarnate life and action He has taken our place, and made us His brothers, and therefore caused us to participate in His life. It is to emphasize this aspect that the New Testament refers to our adoption as sons (Gal. 4:5). We are not members of the family of God by right or nature, nor can we ever be sons of God in the sense of deification. We belong to the family of God by adoption, i.e., as we are brought into relationship with Jesus Christ, and are accepted and recognized as His brothers in virtue of His primary self-identification with us. The divine Fatherhood is not in itself a unifying factor. But when we find our given unity in Christ, we know that we are adopted into the divine family, and therefore have an incontestable and enduring unity in God the Father.

If the concept of adoption keeps before us the truth that

this knowledge of God as the one Father is only in virtue of our unity in Christ as Substitute and Representative, it is balanced by the further concept of regeneration to show that there can be no question of a purely legal recognition. An adopted son may be fully recognized as a son, and have all the rights and privileges of sonship. He may indeed be treated in every respect as a son. Yet the fact remains that he is not really a son, i.e., by generation. Now in our dealings with God this is also true to the extent that we consider our natural life in ourselves. Hence the concept of adoption. But so strict is our identification with Christ, or His identification with us, that in Christ we do really have the life of sons and not merely the status of sons. We are made partakers of the divine nature (II Pet. 1:4). Hence the concept of regeneration (John 3:3, Titus 3:5). Hence, too, the fact that we are united, not merely in the Son and the Father, but also in the Holy Spirit.

In Christ we belong to the divine family by a new birth from above, and not just by a legal pronouncement. This is particularly brought out in the fourth Gospel (John 3:3), but it emerges also in the First Epistle of Peter (1:3), the Epistle of James (1:18), and various Pauline formulations (cf. Gal. 4:19). Birth from above, however, means generation by the one life-giving Spirit (John 3:5). As those who share this new life of the one Spirit, Christians have a real unity, a living and lasting unity, in the Holy Ghost.

Again there is no question of an independent or competitive unity side by side with that which we have in Christ, as though the Spirit Himself were other than the Spirit of Christ, and there were a spiritual life of the community abstracted from its life in Christ. Our birth of the Holy Ghost corresponds, as it were, to Christ's own conception by the Spirit (Luke 1:35), and ultimately to His resurrection by the same Spirit (Rom. 1:4). It is incorporation into the life of Christ, so that we are born into Him and He is born in us. It is a new beginning, first in faith and finally in

resurrection fulfillment, in which there is no longer an autonomous life of self, but Christ Himself is the life of the
Christian (Gal. 2:20, Col. 3:4) by the sovereign action of
the Spirit.   We find our unity in the Spirit because He
is the Spirit of Christ, because He has been at work for us in
Christ Himself incarnate, crucified and risen as our Substitute and Representative, and because He brings us in repentance and faith to the newness of life in which we find
our new and true being in Christ, and express it in our
corresponding movement of death and resurrection (Rom.
6:3ff.) .

The fact that our new birth is spiritual does not mean
that it is isolated from the world of true reality.   It means
that it is of the Holy Spirit.   And that which is done by the
Holy Spirit, in strict relationship to the electing grace of the
Father and the substitutionary activity of the Son, is the
new and true reality now grasped and known in faith and
finally to be revealed in visible triumph and glory.   Already,
as birth to a new life, it necessarily finds its first if sometimes
hesitant expression in new thoughts and words and acts and
attitudes, so that unity in the one Spirit is not merely a
unity of regeneration but a unity of life in which, united in
the one Christ, we are led and impelled by the one Spirit
(Rom. 8:14).   Born of the Spirit, we have a common life in
the Spirit.   To the disunities which still persist in expression
of the carnal and perishing life outside Christ, there is
opposed the indestructible and eternal unity, unrecognized
sometimes but real all the same and demanding recognition,
of all that derives from the one Spirit (Eph. 5:4) .   In so far
as they live in the Spirit, Christians are together; and in
obedience to the Spirit they will necessarily be directed to
the concrete expression of this unity.

Nor is life itself merely an intangible entity.   For although
it is so difficult to define, life means purposeful movement
and action.   Born and living by the one Spirit, Christians
are those who are called and committed to a common task in

the Spirit.   This task may be briefly summed up as the proclamation or showing forth of Jesus Christ as their true life.   It is the witness to Jesus Christ by Word and action. Many things in the lives of Christians may seam to contradict this witness.   But these do not express their true and enduring life in the Spirit.   They are the self-willed irruptions of the old life already replaced in Jesus Christ and by the Holy Spirit.   They are deviations from what is now their only true activity.   In this true activity, however, they are ineluctably one, not by their own self-chosen and reversible commitment to a common creed and enterprise, but by their vital union with Christ and gracious enlistment in the office and work of the Spirit.   They may often fail to realize it. They may even fight against it.   They may make their Christian action an occasion for unholy competition and even conflict.   But in so far as it is genuinely Christian, it can only serve the one purpose and therefore at root be the one action, united for all its external disunities in the Holy Ghost.   And in so far as it is not Christian, it is no longer their true action at all, but a false and futile planning and accomplishing already judged and set aside in Jesus Christ.

Unity in the Spirit, as a unity of life and action, is supremely unity in love.   God is love (I John 4:8).   It is in love (John 3:16) that the Father elects and adopts us in Jesus Christ the Beloved (Eph. 1:6).   It is in love that the Son takes our place and bears away our old and sinful life and gives us new and eternal life in Himself (Gal. 2:20).   It is in love that the Spirit seeks us with the gospel and calls us to Jesus Christ and begets us again in Him, and sets us in our new and true life and activity.   And by the Holy Spirit the love of God is shed abroad in our hearts (Rom. 5:5). Love is the more excellent way (I Cor. 12:31), the supreme gift of the Spirit for every Christian.   Love is the bond of perfectness (Col. 3:14), the royal law (James 2:8), the true and supreme response to the love by which we are first loved

(I John 4:19). United in the Holy Spirit as the Spirit of the Father and the Son, we are united in love.

This does not mean, of course, that we are united by our own emotional or humanitarian impulses. These cannot stand the searching fire of human strife and disruption, and can only lead to bitter disillusionment if we try to find in them unifying substitutes for the love of God. The love in which we are one is ultimately God's own love in His redeeming action as Father, Son, and Spirit. In so far as this is our love, it is by incorporation into Christ, the adoption of the Father and the life-giving operation of the Spirit. That is to say, it is never autonomously, although it is very really ours. And even as ours, in its expression in our own lives, it is primarily love for God (Matt. 22:37). In the unity of the one Spirit of love we are united in love for the one God. And it is because we love God that we are united in love for those who are with us members of Christ's body, brothers in the family of God and fellow recipients of the gifts of the Spirit (I John 4:21).

There is no human route to the true unity of Christian love. It is not an erotic flowering of the old life under the warmth of Christian preaching and the stimulus of common enterprise. It cannot be manufactured by conferences and conventions and conversations. It is not a supreme if rather intangible factor to which appeal can be made on the human level when everything else fails. It is a real unity, contradicting the contradiction of the disunity of jealousy and hatred and anger and bitterness, as the given unity of those who are loved by the one God, and in virtue of His loving action love Him in return, and in so doing are united in love for one another. Unity in love is unity in the Spirit, and therefore in the Father and the Son. As such it is a true and unbreakable and eternal unity on which we can rest, but on which we must also build, in face of the monstrous challenge of disunity in the world or even in the church. The ultimate fact about us as Christians is that we are united in love whatever appearances may say to the contrary. It is here that we must begin, i.e., in Him who first loved us and whom we therefore love. And beginning here, in this real fact, we can move on with confidence and compulsion to our concrete expressions in the Spirit of this imperishable unity of love.

CHAPTER SEVEN

UNITY IN THE DEATH AND RESURRECTION OF CHRIST

———————

WE MUST now take a backward step. In order to show that the unity which we have in Christ is not isolated, but is also a unity in the Father and the Spirit, we have moved away from the central consideration and seen our unity from other aspects. We have still to show, however, the nature of our unification as accomplished in the substitutionary action of the Son, and it is to this more detailed consideration that we must now turn.

As we have seen, the unity of the church is basically its unity in Christ as the One who has taken its place and in whom it has its new and true life. But what does it mean that Christ has taken its place? In what does this unity in Christ consist? What are the elements in the representative life and action of Christ? These questions are of vital importance, not merely for an understanding of the substance of unity, but also for its practical outworking in the life and work of the church.

We may begin by emphasizing that it is a unity in the incarnate life of Christ. The point is not always sufficiently made that the substitutionary work of Christ does not begin with the cross. It begins with the incarnation itself, and therefore with the life of the incarnate Son. Taking the place of men, Jesus lives for them the righteous and obedient life in the flesh which they do not and cannot live for themselves (Heb. 10:7). In His fulfillment of the law, Christians are directed already to the one righteousness which avails for all (cf. Matt. 3:15). Neither to God, themselves, nor the world can they present a varied and perhaps discrepant assortment of human achievements. Their own righteousnesses, however perfect or imperfect, are all superseded by the one righteousness of Christ which is offered to all and must be accepted by all. Everything else is rejected and discarded. They must come to the one Christ for the one righteousness, and therefore they are brought together in Him.

The fact that they meet in the one Christ for their righteousness means, however, that as those who have also to live an incarnate life they are irrevocably bound together in the expression now to be given to this righteousness. That the Christian life is lived, as that of Jesus is seen, in the light of the cross and resurrection, does not mean that it ceases to be a historical life. It is wrong, of course, to try to provide an alternative or additional righteousness or unity by the mere copying of Christ's example or the maintaining of a historical link with his incarnate life. We must be united in His representative righteousness. But the fact that it is a righteousness in the flesh, with genuine historical links, means that it is also to be expressed in the flesh. One in the incarnate righteousness of Christ, we are summoned to conform to this unity in our life in the flesh. We cannot create the unity by our historical action. We find it as we meet in Him. Yet it is in the Incarnate that we meet. And therefore we are to be united in the historical outworking of this representative righteousness and the unity which it gives.

The substitutionary action of Christ consists first in His incarnate life. But the life itself, as a life of obedient righteousness, moves obviously and ineluctably to His death. To see a division between the two, as though we were confronted at this point by an either − or, is wrong and stupid. It is in fulfillment of the law that Jesus enters upon the way of identification with His people which means first the baptism of repentance in Jordan (Matt. 3:15) and finally the baptism of sin-bearing on Calvary (Luke 12:50). Obedience in this substitutionary work means self-offering (Phil. 2:8). The new righteousness is necessarily accompanied by the removal of the old sin. Christ lives for us a human life; but He also dies for us the death of sin. If we are made the righteousness of God in Him, it is only as and because He who knew no sin, as the climax and completion of His sinless life, is made sin for us (II Cor. 5:21).

The death of Christ no less than His life is a substitutionary or representative death. It is the death of the One for the many (Rom. 5:8ff.). But if this is the case, if here, too, Christ is acting in the place and on the behalf of others, this means that we are united with Him in His death. By the fact that He has identified Himself with us, and acted for us, our old life of sin is gathered up as it were and judged and done to death in His death. If one died, then were all dead (II Cor. 5:14). All are crucified in and with Christ (Gal. 2:20). Calvary is the one death of One. But this One is the Mediator for all (I Tim. 2:5). And therefore in Him it is the one death of all. The atoning death of Christ no less than His incarnate life is a focus of unity.

It is this in a twofold sense. In the first place, sinful disunity (as opposed to legitimate diversity) is done to death in Jesus Christ. The victory over disunity as itself an expression of sin is therefore won. It belongs to the old order which still persists but is already defeated and has no future. It yields before the new order of righteousness and righteous unity introduced in the incarnate life of Christ and fulfilled in His resurrection. By the death of the one for the many, the disunity of the many is judged and destroyed, being replaced by their unity in the One.

But there is a second sense in which the death of Christ is a focus of unity. For if all sinners must come to the incarnate Christ for their righteousness, they must come to the crucified Christ for the judgment and therefore the forgiveness of their sin. It is indicative of the unifying power of the cross that the most diverse and divided of sinners are united in the encompassing of the death of Christ. Pilate and Herod and Caiaphas and Judas are all agreed on this. Of itself, however, this gives us merely the hopeless truth that for all their disunity even sinners are ultimately united in their sin. The deeper and more comforting and positive truth to which this points is that they are not just united in the old Adam (Rom. 5:12) in bringing about the death of the new, but that they are also united in the new Adam dying the death of the old. With all their divisions and conflicts they come together in the one Son of God and Man who takes the place of sinners and does away their sin and therefore their division. They all die on the one cross. They are all buried in the one grave (Rom. 6:3ff.). The many sinful and divided selves all meet, as they are all destroyed, in the one Sin-bearer. And therefore in death, i.e., in the death of Christ which is also their death, they are already united.

The fact that they meet in the one Christ for their judgment and destruction means, however, that as those who have also to die to sin they are irrevocably bound together in the expression to be given to this dying. The historical life which we now live is a life moving to its end and therefore a life under the cross. United in the cross of Christ, we are also united in the fact that we have to bear our cross, denying the old self and finding our new life in Christ (Mark 8:34f.). This does not mean that we have a variety of additional or alternative crosses alongside that of Jesus. We must be united in His death. But this unity is to find expression in our dying to self in all our thought and speech and action, whether in individual life or in that of the church. One in the cross of Christ, we are summoned to conform to this unity in our common mortification

(Eph. 4:22). We cannot create this unity, e.g., by calling ourselves or others to acts of repentance. We find it as we meet in the Crucified, taking up our own crosses only as and because we are already found on His cross. But we do really meet in the Crucified, and therefore we are to be united in the outworking of this representative death and the unity which we are given as those who know that in Him it is we who were crucified at Golgotha.

Yet obviously it is not enough to meet in death. It may well be true that in this death sin is done away, and therefore there need be no fear either of its further action or its penalties and consequences. Yet death itself is surely the triumph of sin. And unity in death is merely a unity in disintegration and therefore no final answer to the challenge of disunity. It is arguable, perhaps, that even if God's reconciling action had ended in the tomb sin and disunity would have been destroyed and a certain unity established. But fortunately this is mere speculation. The incarnate and crucified Christ could not remain the buried Christ, and therefore on the third day God raised Him from the dead (Acts 2:24). But the resurrection of Christ no less than His incarnation and crucifixion was a representative and substitutionary resurrection. Hence the fact that the One is risen means that the many are risen in and with Him. United in the Incarnate and the Crucified, they are also and supremely united in the Resurrected. The new and true life of all is supremely the life which is hid with Christ in God (Col. 3:3). And this life, as life in the One, is one life.

It is this because a life of unity is brought in to replace the scattered and divided lives which we live in ourselves and which are done away in the death of Christ. The new order has now come to replace the old. The old has not merely been vanquished. It has been victoriously superseded. Nor has it been superseded merely by a unity in death. It has been superseded by a unity in eternal life. Whatever may seem to be the power of disunity in the present age, it does not and cannot have the last word. For the real life of the church is now its one life in the resurrected Christ. This reality of unity has already been introduced in His vicarious resurrection, and there is awaited only its triumphant manifestation with the last day.

But again, Christians meet as they come to Jesus Christ for their new life. They do not go their separate ways to their separate resurrections. They come to the Resurrected and find their one resurrection in Him. If they, too, are to be raised, it is only on the basis and in the power of the one resurrection. Those who live already in Christ can no longer live to themselves. They can live only to the One who is risen in their place and in whom they have their life (II Cor. 5:15). And since they all live in and to Him, they are all bound the one to the other. This does not mean only that they are bound to one another by a common belief and hope. It has the stricter meaning that they are brought together in the One who has taken the place of all, and died and risen again in that place and therefore for them. Hence they cannot escape this unity of life unless they refuse to accept Jesus Christ as their life, and therefore refuse to be Christians.

But the fact that they meet in the one Christ for resurrection and life means that as those who are also to be raised they are irrevocably committed to a common expression of renewal. The historical life which they now live is not merely a life under the cross but a life under the promise of renewal. It is thus a life in which there are to be shown already the marks of the new life which is already the true life of the church. There is a certain ambivalence here. As those who are regenerate with Christ, Christians are in a very real sense following the pattern of the incarnation. They cannot, then, live as those whose own resurrection has already come, or regard their life in Christ as one which is remote and future and in this sense a refuge from everyday reality. Yet they are also resurrected with Christ (Col.

3:1), so that their common life in Him must bear not only the marks of incarnation and mortification but also of renewal. They cannot create this unity in renewal, e.g., by the conscious attempts to bind the churches together in a spiritual awakening. They find it as they meet in the Resurrected, being renewed as they enter into their renewal in Him. But they do really meet in Him. They are therefore to be united in the outworking of this representative resurrection and the unity which we are given as those who know that in Him it is we who were raised the third day from the dead.

The fact that this unity of the church is a unity in resurrection is the guarantee of its triumph against all divisive and disintegrating factors. God Himself has put forth His creative power to bind His people together in a unity which is dynamic, inviolable, and eternal. But the fact that it is a unity in the resurrection of Christ is the guarantee that it is not merely a hope for the future, but a reality which is already present. Christian realism does not underestimate the power of disunity. But it finds it outmatched by the divine power of unity already put forth in the life and death and supremely the resurrection of Jesus Christ. It can therefore address itself to the challenge of disunity with the confidence that the definitive victory is already won, that a solid indicative underlies the imperative, that the church has only to be what it is, that the temporal reality of division must yield, however reluctantly, to the eternal and living reality of unity.

CHAPTER EIGHT

THE PATTERN OF UNITY

———

WE HAVE NOW REJECTED false or inadequate ways of conceiving Christian unity. We have pointed instead to the place where it is genuinely to be found, namely, in the incarnate, crucified, and risen Christ and therefore in the Father and the Holy Spirit. We may now turn to the more practical task of examining the forms or subsidiary foci of unity in the provisional concretions which it must find in the church. But in so doing it is necessary that we should not suddenly swerve aside from the truth already gained, or arbitrarily follow a plan of our own choosing, as though any structure could be built on this foundation. We may, therefore, review our findings with a view to discerning the pattern of unity as it must guide us in all our attempted fulfillments.

In the first instance, it is obviously a unity of faith (Eph. 4:5). This does not mean a unity of dogmatic tenets, to which we shall have to return later. Nor does it mean that faith creates the unity. It is the object of faith which creates the unity, namely, the one Christ acting on our behalf. But the fact remains that faith, itself a work of God, is the means by which we apprehend our unity in Christ. And therefore in its practical expression unity will manifest itself in a common faith. Christians are one, first because they are gathered together in Jesus Christ, but secondly and in consequence because they believe in the one

Savior and Lord. Even in respect of this latter unity, it is to be remarked that it is not self-created. But it consists in a definite human action and attitude in response to the call of Jesus and the inward moving of the Spirit. It is evoked and nurtured by definite means of grace, i.e., the word and sacraments and the ministry, and it finds expression in a definite action of confession, discipleship, and service. The church is one in its one faith in the one Lord, its one use of the common means of grace and its one dedication to the common task.

Second, it is no less obviously a unity of what we might call incarnational duality. Believing in the Christ who took flesh for them, Christians realize that as those who are born from above they have to give a reflection or refraction of the incarnate life and work of Christ. They are left in the world as the representatives of the One who is their great Representative. They cannot create unity in this common discipleship. It is not a self-subsistent unity, just as their "incarnation" is not a self-subsistent and therefore alternative or additional incarnation. The unity itself is there in Christ. But because it is a unity in Christ incarnate, it brings them together in giving it historical concretion during the period that they remain on earth, and the old order endures. The church is one in the sense that, finding the reality of unity in the incarnate Christ, it necessarily bears itself the marks of an analogous duality.

This means, however, that it is committed to giving its life, and therefore its unity, historical shape. The church is always a historical entity. It cannot cease to be this during the time between the ascension and the return of Christ. Indeed, we may conclude that even in the last resurrection, when it is clothed upon by a new and glorious and perfect body, it will still reflect the incarnational duality of Christ. But for the moment it does so in terms of the old and mortal and sinful life. It cannot be either a purely spiritual society on the one side or merely an ecclesiastical association on the other. It is a colony of heaven, but it works itself out in the forms of religion and ecclesiastical organization. And for all the disunity and variety, it is always more or less recognizably the one entity of the church of Christ, grouped around the one Bible, making the one confession, engaged in the same task of preaching and administering the sacraments, giving itself to the same ministry of proclamation and worship. Indeed, even within the enduring historical entities, it is commonly committed to the giving of individual forms to its life in response to the remorseless pressure of time and circumstance. It may be very far from one in the structure and detailed forms of its historical being. But beyond the variety there remains a unity of reflected incarnation which is a necessary mark of the church, which gives it its common task in the present sphere, and which provides an enduring impulse to unity as well as the possibility of its achievement.

Third, the unity of the church is equally obviously a unity of death and resurrection. Giving themselves to the common discipleship of Jesus Christ, Christians are commonly engaged to follow the way which leads to Calvary and the empty tomb. Here again it is not their common will for discipleship which creates the unity. It is not that they themselves die and rise again which makes them one. But their unity in the death and resurrection of the One whom they believe and follow brings them together in activity which is marked always by dying and renewal. The church which is true to its Lord, and therefore to itself, is the church which is ready to go this way, which sees its whole expression of Christian life in this world as only temporary and provisional, which is prepared for the constant criticism and renewal of its historical forms, which does not absolutize itself, which does not try to evade or resist the cross, but which bears always in its life the dying and therefore the rising again of its Master. United on Good Friday and Easter Day, Christians are genuinely at one, for all their disunities, to the extent that they follow the pattern which this entails.

This unity of death and resurrection is primarily spiritual. Perhaps the greatest obstacle to genuine unity in the church is the basic unwillingness of the old man to die, his clinging to what he thinks is good and valuable at least in himself as a Christian, his refusal of the way of the cross and his consequent perpetuation in inward and outward disunity. But on the basis of their unity in the death and resurrection of Christ Christians are called insistently and unceasingly to the common losing of their own lives that they might find them as the one life. Yet it is also a theological unity. There is a common apprehension that our present life is only temporary. The church militant as a whole must become the church triumphant. The general movement is to death, and through death to resurrection. Unitedly engaged in its expression of the "incarnation," the church has a common understanding that as the body of Christ it, too, must go to the cross even in respect of that which is a more adequate reflection, let alone in respect of its follies and failures. It is marked by the same baptismal sign and committed to the same road, so that even when it is blind and rebellious the fact of this unity is secure. But it also comes together in its treading of this road, and in its ultimate awareness that it cannot finally avoid it. Finally, it is a practical unity, more particularly in relation to the forms in which the church manifests its historical entity. For all its attempts to preserve them, these forms are subject to the ineluctable movements and pressures of chance and change, so that willy-nilly the church is committed to a constant process of destruction and renewal. To be sure, this is true of all life. But on the basis of the death and resurrection of Christ the church is brought together in seeing why it is true, and in accepting the challenge which it brings. Not all the church's life is to be abandoned to the relativities of history. There are things which remain so long as earthly life remains, i.e., the basic patterns of ministry and worship. But the forms which these things take cannot and must not be absolutized, or the church refuses the way of discipleship and is thus condemned to disunity. At every point and in every respect the way of discipleship is the way of death and resurrection, and Christians united in the death and resurrection of Christ are brought together in their common acceptance of this way.

Finally, the unity of the church is obviously a unity of ministry. Giving historical concretion to its life in Christ and therefore moving to death and resurrection, it does so in a common act of service to Christ and to the world. Again, the common task or dedication does not create the unity. A common purpose, like a common belief or manner of life, can be a powerful unifying factor. But the unity here goes deeper. It is to be found in the ministry of Christ Himself on behalf of the church. If the church has a ministry, it is not an independent ministry, but one which rests upon the basic ministry of Christ. It is the declaring of His all-sufficient work to the world. And if it is united in this task, the unity is not created by its own willingness or fulfillment, but by the Lord Himself, by the work which He Himself has done and the commission which He Himself has given. Yet the fact remains that unity in Christ means also unity in the acceptance and fulfillment of the ministry which He enjoins. The church has its analogous incarnation, and goes to its analogous death and resurrection, in pursuance of its analogous mission. Its genuine unity will and must always be a unity of service; and in giving itself to its service it will and must always find its unity.

In the discharge of its service, as in the evoking and nurturing of its faith, the expression of its life and indeed its summoning to death and resurrection, the church makes use of constant historical factors fashioned and adapted to serve this very purpose, i.e., the word of God in the

Bible, the confession of Christ, the sacraments, and the ministry. These factors are not exempt from the ultimate transformation which the church itself is to undergo. In their detailed forms, they, too, are subject to a constant process of reformation and renewal. But for the practical outworking of the unity of the church as a unity of faith, of incarnational duality, of death and resurrection, and above all perhaps of ministry, they have a particular importance which entitles us to see in them essential factors and subsidiary foci of unity, and to refer to them in our discussion of the practical program which should result from our consideration of the basis and pattern of unity.

It must be underlined, however, that these factors are not the basis. This is to be found in the substitutionary work of Christ and therefore the reconciling action of the Trinity. Again, they do not give us the pattern of unity. This derives from the Holy Spirit calling the church to faith, to historical concretion, to death and resurrection, and to its common ministry. We cannot say, then, that we have here the primary essentials or foci of unity. But if they are not the basis or pattern and therefore not the primary foci, they are the means or orders divinely appointed and used for the calling of the church to its life and unity, and therefore subsidiary foci. What makes the church the church, and therefore the one church, is the work of Christ and conformity under the Holy Spirit to this work. But if it is this church, it will be the church which in some form and measure profits by and exercises these orders and means. We blunder seriously if we try to make the means, and even more so an individual form of the means, the ground or standard of the church's life or unity. But we also blunder if we do not give them their real importance in the practical expression of the unity achieved in Christ and the outworking of the given pattern.

In the chapters which follow, as we try to see how the triumphant unity achieved in Christ can express itself in practical conquests of disunity, we shall take these means as the guiding foci of discussion and proposal. We shall remember, of course, that they serve only to give provisional actualization to a unity already attained, and that they can do this only as they help to promote a common pattern. They neither achieve the unity on the one side, nor do they dictate its pattern on the other. But in virtue of their divine appointment and use they can and should serve the expression of what is already achieved according to the pattern of its achievement. It is with this proper estimate of their importance and office, and the awareness that otherwise they are far more calculated to foment disunity, that we now turn to them for guidance in the outworking of unity according to a true and christological pattern.

CHAPTER NINE

UNITY AND THE BIBLE

Of the means and subsidiary foci of unity the Bible is the first and most obvious and perhaps the most important. With very few exceptions, all churches are agreed in acceptance of the Bible as a basic standard of faith and practice. Even where it is imagined that special illuminations can replace the Bible, there remains an essential biblical content unless the Christian faith is completely abandoned. Again, even in new churches on the mission field, which do not yet have the Bible in their own tongues and perhaps rely to a great extent on the spoken word, the Bible underlies the whole enterprise of faith and discipleship, and the word of preaching and teaching is a biblical word. It is perhaps going a little too far to make acceptance of the Bible an absolute standard of unity or communion, but in view of its overriding importance the Bible is plainly essential to the unity and indeed to the whole life and being of the church, both as a focus on the one side and a means on the other. If the church is ultimately united in Christ, it is united around the Bible which speaks of Christ.

On the other hand, we have to recognize that the Bible is also a fruitful source of dissension and disunity in and among the churches, so that acceptance of its authority does not solve at once the problem of unity. There is disagreement, for instance, concerning the actual constitution of the Bible, some contending for greater comprehension and others for greater exclusion. The interpretation of the Bible gives rise to a whole series of more or less important and divisive differences. The doctrine of the Bible and its inspiration and authority is another cause of dissension, especially when it is contended by some that the Bible is only one standard of life and faith among others. Minor differences can even arise concerning the particular translations of the Bible to be used; and indeed this is a significant issue in the whole relationship of Romanist and non-Romanist churches. These are obviously very real difficulties which cannot be ignored even if they cannot be fully faced and answered. We have to ask, therefore, how the Bible can be a true focus and means of unity in the practical relationships of the churches when even in this sphere there is the constant bias to disunity.

Now in the first place we must remember that the Bible is not to be abstracted from Christ and made a center of unity in its own right. This is important for two reasons. The first is the negative one that we make unity impossible if we insist that all Christians and churches must begin by accepting the Bible, or even a particular view of the nature or constitution of the Bible, as a proof of their genuine Christianity. The second is the positive one that unity is grounded in Christ Himself, and that it is served by the Bible when the Bible is understood in clear relationship to Christ as the authoritative prophetic and apostolic testimony. We may go to the Bible with very different views of what it is and how it is to be understood or applied. But if we go primarily to see Christ (John 5:39), i.e., to learn what the Bible has to tell us about Him, and our new life in Him, we shall be brought together at the one true center of the church and its unity.

This leads us to the further thought, however, that the Bible, too, shows something of the incarnational duality of Christ, both in its origin as inspired by the Holy Ghost yet written by men, and also in its present being as a book which remains the same under forms which continually vary. For the moment it is the second of these two points which claims our attention. When we take the Bible as a means and focus of unity, we think of an enduring entity of the Old and New Testament Scriptures, yet we cannot identify it absolutely with any particular version or copy. There is scope for a multiplicity of better and worse translations or presentations in response to changing historical and geographical needs. The Hebrew and Greek remain the ultimate norms, but since in the good providence of God we do not have the originals even these cannot be withdrawn from the relativities of history. One of the greatest stumbling blocks to unity in this field is when a particular rendering, e.g., the Vulgate, is given an absolute status, or the attempt is made to prevent the free publication of Scripture in living and changing tongues.

If this is true of the text, it is equally true of our understanding of the text. There is a very real sense, of course, in which the insights of the past remain. And scriptural truth itself is constant. Yet it has to be recalled that Christians are like householders bringing new as well as old things out of their treasures. It is the privilege of different ages to see biblical truth in new ways or from new angles or with a new relevance, not reading in or drawing out what is not there, nor imagining that they are developing or improving the teaching of the writers, but being led by the Holy Spirit into a new appreciation of the enduring witness to Christ. This means that in the exposition of the Bible there must be the genuine humility which may often mean a dying and rising again such as that which Luther underwent when he came to see the real meaning of the righteousness of God. To insist rigidly upon a particular exegesis or doctrinal formulation because it is traditional or individual, thus closing the way to any possibility of reformation, is to make of the Bible a false center of unity, and an inevitable source of disunity.

The Bible is given us, of course, for the pursuance of the

church's ministry, whether in the edification of existing believers or in the calling of new ones. It is not to be a remote and unused entity above the ordinary life of Christians. If the place which it occupies is one of particular importance, it is naturally a place within the general ministry of the church. It will not unify, therefore, merely, as a book about which certain things are to be believed but very little done. It will unify as it is used for the purpose for which it was given, namely, as an instrument of ministering Christ to the people. This brings us back again to our first point, that the Bible must not be abstracted from Christ Himself. It will not be a means or focus of unity merely in virtue of the fact that we are all trying to present biblical truth. But it will certainly be this as we are all trying to present Christ Himself as the Truth attested in the Bible. In relationship to the primary focus, and caught up in the ministry of reconciliation which in its own way the church shares with its incarnate, crucified, and risen Head, it can and will serve as a true subsidiary focus.

When we come to practical suggestions for the promotion of unity through the Bible, the first is quite simply that the Bible should always be seen in this relationship to Christ Himself and the given unity which there is in Him. Otherwise it can only be a center of division. It may well be true that different readers come with different ideas of Christ, or derive different impressions. There is a constant need of correction as we come to this apostolic and authoritative record. But if we come to find Christ, and are ready to learn of Him, we shall be drawn together in our reading of the Bible for all the variety in our detailed understanding.

Second, there is required a readiness to accept the free movement of scholarship in respect of textual criticism on the one side and translation on the other. In other words, we are not to insist that one particular version is the only real Bible, but to give ourselves to the common task of pro-

viding new and better versions. Difficulties obviously arise
in this connection. Can we strain the legitimate and necessary freedom to the point of allowing the addition of the
apocrypha by some, the publication of very dubious or even
false renderings by others, the excision of disliked passages
by others? What are we to say in face of those who themselves claim an absolutely authoritative rendering?   Well,
we obviously cannot endorse every rendering or edition, and
we must be at pains to state our objections.   But so long as
the core of the Bible remains we need not spring too readily
to sweeping excommunications.   And if we are excommuni-
cated by others who insist upon their particular rendering,
we can quietly pursue our way, making common cause with
them in the study of the underlying Greek and Hebrew, and
leaving it for time to show that there must always be new
versions in accordance with changing circumstances.   More
positively, however, we must combine wherever possible with
other Christians to produce worthy renderings either in our
own tongue or in that of other peoples, accepting the common discipline of effort and scholarship which this imposes.

Third, there is required a constant discussion in the field
of biblical exposition, not only between the churches but between individual scholars and teachers within and among
the churches. Much of this work may well be futile. Much
of it may be conducted with a view to scholastic ends rather
than those of genuine exposition. Much of it may fail to
come from Christ, and therefore to lead to Him. Much of
it may cause sharp division not merely between but even
within the churches. But it is a necessary task in which all
can and should combine even across the normal barriers of
denominational loyalty. And in so far as there is a genuine
desire to see Christ, and a readiness to expound what is really in the Bible, the task of exposition promotes a unity
including but transcending the comradeship of those engaged
in a common enterprise.

Finally, the Bible poses the common task of making it

known to our own and every nation, whether in the form of the text itself or the truth which it embodies. This includes, of course, the necessary work of translation and the continuing task of exposition, which belong to the ministry of the church. It is part of the whole task of the church, namely, the presenting of Christ Himself as the one Mediator between God and man. And it is a part of the task in which in different ways and according to their different understandings all professing Christians are constantly engaged. Indeed, it is a part which itself claims the attention of all Christian bodies, for where in the church has the reading of the Bible failed altogether, however imperfect or unfruitful? Do we not all wish to proclaim the Christ, and to proclaim Him as He is attested in Scripture, even though our different understandings may lead us to do this in very different ways?

The fact that this is so has led many different churches with very different confessions to come together in the printing and publishing and distribution of Scripture in many different lands and countries. This work of the Bible Societies is a genuine example of ecumenical action in the unity of ministry around the common center of the Bible, and it is a work which might bring the churches even closer together if they were to apply themselves to it even more wholeheartedly and accept its principles in wider spheres, e.g., of biblical exegesis and theology. Here, at any rate, the unity in Christ, finding a subsidiary means and focus, works itself out, not in mere talk, but in a positive task of proclamation and instruction. Nor does this merely serve the primary task of bringing others to Christ and nurturing them in Him. It binds together those who engage in the enterprise. It stimulates to parallel activity even those who remain outside. It points the way to similar action in other biblical spheres. And it is an indication of the practical attainment of unity which is possible in even wider areas when Christ Himself is set in the forefront, when the church gives itself to self-sacrificial ministry in the conditions of its time, and when a proper approach is made of the means and foci of unity which God Himself has ordained and maintains and uses in the church.

What does all this amount to in terms of a general program of unity? We may summarize it as follows. The churches can and should unite in seeking and teaching Christ in the Scriptures. They can and should unite in providing reliable versions for their own use and that of others. They can and should unite in biblical study, both in the wider field of interdenominational scholarship and in the humbler and more local spheres of groups for the study and understanding and application of the Bible. They can and should continue and strengthen their united endeavor to give the Bible to the nations in the cause of evangelism and edification. They cannot create unity by adopting and carrying through a program of this kind, nor can they evade the pressures of disunity. But in and by it they can express the unity which they already have in their common Lord, and gain provisional but important victories over the forces which disrupt and divide them.

CHAPTER TEN

UNITY AND CONFESSION

AT A FIRST GLANCE it might not appear that the confession of faith is quite in the same category as the Bible as something which God Himself has appointed to be a constant and constituent factor in the church. A little thought, however, will show that in its own place and manner confession is undoubtedly a factor of this kind and therefore a means and focus of unity. In His incarnate presence among men Jesus Christ evoked confession with His question to the disciples: "Whom say ye that I am?" (Matt. 16:15). When He was risen from the dead, His appearance and challenge to Thomas produced the confession: "My Lord and my God" (John 20:24f.). When the disciples first preached, they summoned the people to call on the name of the Lord (Acts 2:21), and Philip stirred the eunuch to the confession: "I believe that Jesus Christ is the Son of God" (Acts 8:37). Paul summed it up clearly in Romans (10:10): "For with the heart man believeth unto righteousness; and with the mouth confession is made unto salvation." The importance of confession is that it expresses the response of faith to Jesus Christ proclaimed in the Bible, summing up the biblical message in terms of the believer's answer. As such, it belongs naturally and necessarily to the nature of the church and the life of its members.

The fact that all Christian bodies confess in some way their faith in Jesus Christ, whether in a simple affirmation or in the expanded form of the creeds, is obviously a uni-

fying factor in the midst of division. The majority of Protestant churches, for example, can join hands with the Roman
and Eastern Orthodox in saying the great creeds which embody the Christian faith in the triune God and His saving
work in Jesus Christ. Even those who might stumble at
individual phrases, e.g., in the Nicene or Athanasian creeds,
can confess that Jesus Christ is Savior and Lord. For all
the differences which arise in detailed beliefs, the Christian
community as a whole presents a more or less united front
to the world in its basic confession; and perhaps it is not
always sufficiently realized that these fundamental beliefs
which unite are no less, and perhaps greater, than the beliefs which separate.

Yet the confession, like the Bible, can be an instrument
of disunity as well as unity. Even the very simplest affirmation that Jesus Christ is Lord (I Cor. 12:3) can (rightly)
mark off those who wish to follow Jesus on their own terms
but not on His. An expansion like the Apostles' Creed is
obviously adapted to exclude those who hold erroneous
teachings in relation to individual aspects of faith, and with
the continual development of creeds and statements of faith
to express belief on individual points the process of disruption is obviously accelerated. Christians of many allegiances
may perhaps come together in the basic affirmations, but
when they present their detailed confessions of faith they
are at once plunged into more or less bitter and hopeless
contention. Nor does this apply only to the great divisions
between Roman, Orthodox, and Protestant. It applies
equally to the lesser but important differences within Protestantism, e.g., between Lutherans and Reformed, Armin-
ians and Calvinists, Baptists and Paedobaptists, etc. Not
every difference is regarded as a ground of actual division
by every body, but schisms innumerable have taken place
for detailed points of confession, and the "infallible" pro-
nouncements of the Pope make any genuine unity in con-

fession almost impossible so far as the Roman communion is concerned.

If the confession is to be a genuine means and focus of unity, the first essential is to see it in its proper function as a response of faith to Jesus Christ. This means that it is not the ground of unity. Nor is it an instrument for the testing of orthodoxy. Nor is it a guarantee of unity in accepted and infallible dogma. In the first instance, confession is simply the expression of a genuine but perhaps very imperfect and ill-instructed faith in Jesus Christ. It is Jesus Christ who saves and unites, not our beliefs about Him or the expression which we give to these beliefs. To abstract the confession from Jesus Christ as an independent ground or guarantee of unity or catholicity is to turn it from its true function, to pervert the faith which it is designed to state, and to introduce inevitable dissension. To be sure, Jesus Christ must be accepted and confessed as the One He is, i.e., the Savior and Lord. But in confession we must never lose sight of the fact that it is He whom we are confessing, not our detailed beliefs concerning Him, and that even though we may differ widely in our doctrine and interpretation we are united in our faith in Him.

This brings us to a second point, that although confession of Jesus Christ is constant the form which it may assume at different times and in different places is variable, not merely in the language used, but even in the actual expression. Prior to the great councils not all churches used a single creed, and while the Apostles' Creed obviously summarizes the content of the gospel there is nothing sacrosanct about the selection of individual words or statements. If this is true about the ancient creeds, it is even more true about the more elaborate confessions in which churches have felt it is necessary to state their mind on disputed issues. An Anglican, for example, might well feel that certain doctrines enumerated in the Thirty-Nine Articles are true as opposed to the false conceptions of Trent. But he cannot say that all

Christians must express them in this way. He cannot claim that this particular confession can never be improved or amended in the light of biblical teaching. He cannot insist that all Christians must think as he does on these matters or else they cannot be regarded as Christians at all. He recognizes that when we come to the confessions of beliefs we enter the sphere of relative human statement and therefore of constant scrutiny and reformation.

But does this mean that unity can persist even where there is error? Does not genuine unity have to be unity in truth? Can we cooperate with other Christian bodies when we are convinced that on certain issues they think and speak falsely? This is a difficulty which is felt acutely by almost all Christians except those who are so vague in their own convictions that they can extend an easy hand of comprehension to all parties, and fail to understand them when it is rejected. On the one hand there are Roman Catholics who insist that every defined dogma is necessary to eternal salvation except in cases of invincible ignorance. On the other there are Evangelicals who break off relationship over minute points, e.g., of prophetic interpreation. Between these are the great confessions which feel that a line must be drawn at this or that place because the truth of the gospel itself is brought into question. Is there any means of preserving or restoring unity in confession in face of this obvious difficulty?

The starting-point is that unity in truth, as in righteousness, cannot mean unity in our own apprehension of truth or attainment of righteousness. Otherwise we should be condemned to constant unity in untruth. It means unity in the Truth, namely, Jesus Christ Himself. To confess Jesus Christ as the Truth, as Savior and God, is to be brought into an indestructible unity of confession even though there may be the widest variations in our apprehension of what is involved. Even within our confessing churches we always have Christians at different levels of apprehension and sometimes with the most glaring heresies of ignorance or self-opinion. Yet in the one confession of the one Christ we are all engaged in the common task of learning and understanding. And if this is true of individuals within individual churches, it is no less true of the churches themselves in their attempts at more detailed confession. To confess Jesus Christ as Savior and Lord is obviously essential. To accept an intricate definition of His relationship to God is not so obviously essential to saving faith, and surely ought not to be imposed as a condition of unity.

Yet there has to be a working out of the truth, as of righteousness, in the power of the Spirit and under the standard of Scripture. To this extent there is a real justification for more elaborate confessions; and in many cases the truths which they embody seem no less necessary to the evangelical life of the church than moral standards to its ethical. Thus, even though we realize that we are no more saved by beliefs than our works, but only by faith in Christ, are we not constrained to make a firm stand for what seem to be clear and biblical doctrines? And even if we are prepared to accept as Christians those who think otherwise, do we not have to dissociate ourselves from their errors and therefore pursue a different path of preaching and teaching? Is there any way out of the resultant *impasse* for our relationships with other confessions?

Unless we cling to the fact that unity is in Christ as the Truth and our confession of Him rather than in our statements of truth, there is obviously no possible way. All who think differently on important issues must be expelled or abandoned or denounced, and the fallibility of man defies the given unity in Christ in a riot of dogmatic disruption. But if we take seriously the fact that we are united in Christ, and therefore in the Truth, and therefore in our basic confession, there is a hard way that can be taken to overcome the doctrinal difficulties. It begins in humility, i.e., the recognition by each Christian and Christian body that it must be reformable under the Word and Spirit of God. It leads by way of evangelistic concern, namely, that Christ must be presented and souls won to Him, not only in our own christianized lands but also in distant continents, even though important points are still under dispute. It involves a readiness to learn and teach in mutual prayer and discussion even where there seems at first very little to learn and no great hope of teaching. It is guided always by an ultimate loyalty to Scripture, so that in the last resort nothing will be demanded but that which is actually written in the terms in which it is written, and this by way of a spiritual rather than an intellectual demand. It will be informed by understanding and charity, i.e., the recognition that heresy is only another expression of the old man, and that if there is a plain requirement to overcome the error there is an equally plain requirement to help the one who is guilty of it. It is not a question of appeasement or compromise. It is a question of our quiet acceptance of the unity in Christ of all who confess His name, and a common commitment to the humble and patient task of understanding the implications of confession as the Bible declares them.

What does this mean in practice? In other words, how can it work itself out in a united church in this or that particular country? In the first place, there is naturally entailed a common confession of Christ as Savior and Lord; and Christians may and should begin now by acceptance of the confession which they all make, whether in baptism or a form of confirmation or attested decision. Second, there must be a concentration upon the common preaching and teaching of positive biblical truth. Third, the common deposit of faith, e.g., in the Apostles' Creed, is to be accepted, but with no prescription of use or enforcement of rigid conformity. Fourth, opportunity must be given for the free and patient and continuing discussion, orally and in writing, of all disputed issues, without rancor or scorn or self-will or threats or repression, but with a common desire to learn and teach

in the school of Christ. Fifth, different and even contradictory confessions must be taken into the common body for
continual scrutiny, reformation, and attempted reconciliation under the Word of God. Sixth, minority opinions
are to be respected, although with a hope of final resolution,
so long as preaching and teaching are not made an occasion
for mere propaganda but subordinated to the positive task
of evangelism and edification.

It need hardly be said that the tensions involved in such
a program would make it impossible of realization were it
not for the basic unity in the confession of the one Lord,
the recognition that the one faith find expression in changing
and reformable formulations and the common acceptance
of the pattern of dying and rising again in Christian thinking no less than Christian living, i.e., the bringing of every
thought into captivity to Christ. We may emphasize, however, that equally essential to the practical realization of
this program is the clear and insistent perception that confession, too, is part of the ministry of the church. The point
of confession is not merely to assure others that we believe,
or to satisfy our own longing for expression, or to give an
assurance of orthodoxy, but to proclaim Christ to the world
in an act of clear and grateful acknowledgment. In other
words, confession is testimony. This means that it is finally
positive. It means, too, that it belongs to the service which
is a mark of genuine unity and in which the church is
united. Far too often confession is narrowly conceived of
as a matter of internal relationship and discipline. What
Christians and Christian bodies have to see is that in confession they engage in a common proclamation of their common Lord and Savior to a world which does not yet know
and trust Him as He really is. They may frankly admit to
one another and to the world that there are many things
which they do not properly understand and cannot state in
concert. But if they really know and confess Christ as Son
of God and Savior, they must come and stand together as

one confessing body to give to the world and themselves the one testimony to the one Christ, and to win the world and themselves, not to the acceptance of a uniform system of belief, but to common faith in Him.

CHAPTER ELEVEN

UNITY AND THE SACRAMENTS

CLOSELY BOUND UP with the Bible on the one side and confession on the other are the sacramental actions of baptism and the Lord's Supper which have come down from New Testament days and are still continued in almost all sections of the Christian church. As it is God who has given us the Bible, and evoked our confession, so it is the Lord who has instituted these two actions, not only by His command (Matt. 28:19, Luke 22:19), but also by His example (Matt. 3:13ff., 26:26ff.). They are thus continuing factors in the life of the church in time, and as such may rightly be regarded as means and foci for the outworking of the church's unity.

The mere fact that the majority of Christian communions have these two signs in common is in itself a unifying factor of great importance. Of different ages and background, with different outlooks and beliefs and customs, those who confess Christ in response to the biblical word all stand under the same sign and meet in the one act of table fellowship. For all their diversity and disunity they may be recognized as the one family in their obedient fulfillment of the Lord's commands. We can hardly say that those who for different reasons refuse to make use of the sacraments disqualify themselves as Christians. But we can at least say that the visible church is a company of faithful men where the sacraments are duly administered.

Yet here again, and no less powerfully, we are faced by

the fact that the sacraments can also be instruments of disunity. This may take place in many different ways. It may be because some argue that there are other sacraments equally necessary to the life and character of the church. It may be because there is insistence that they must be administered according to a certain pattern, or on the assumption of a particular understanding of their meaning and efficacy. It may be by the non-recognition of the sacraments as given in other bodies, or the exclusion of this or that group from sacramental administration. In this sphere, as in that of the Bible, it seems as though the problems raised by the means and focus of unity are greater than the benefits conferred; and that if we are to wait for a solution to all these problems there is little hope of any practical attainment of unity.

Now it is important that the problems raised should be faced and answered. But it is no less important that this should take place within the united church rather than outside it, i.e., that the sacraments should be allowed to exercise their unifying influence even while discussion takes place for their better administration and understanding. Nor is it necessary to achieve unanimity in order that this may happen. The only prerequisite is that the sacraments should not be made independent foci of unity, but brought into relationship with the pattern of unity as already discerned and applied in other fields.

In the first place, it must be seen that the sacraments are genuinely dominical sacraments, attesting and promoting the unity which there is in Christ. It is not merely that they derive from the one Lord and are therefore common acts of obedience, though this is also significant. The real point is that they are witnesses to the one baptism and cup of the cross which gives an underlying and unshakable unity to our many baptisms and cups. The real point is that, whatever the form and understanding, we are baptized into Christ and are nourished by Him. We obviously make unity impossible if or to the extent that we abstract the sacraments from Christ Himself. But when we see them in relationship to Him, they can serve as means and foci of unity because they attest the one Christ and His one work, thus drawing us to Him and in Him to one another.

Again, the sacraments clearly reflect the incarnational duality of Christ, not only in their ultimate essence and efficacy, but also in their continued use in the church. They consist of enduring actions: washing with water in the triune name, and the taking of bread and wine in remembrance of Christ's broken body and blood. But these actions can be understood in different ways and carried out in very different forms, varying from the starkest simplicity to the most elaborate ceremonial. In answer to the different needs of different ages and peoples there is no reason whatever why there should not be variety in administration so long as the essentials remain (the Romanist denial of the cup to the laity is a very serious violation in this respect) and scriptural norms are followed. The unity does not lie in the form adopted, but in the basic action as an obedient witness to the one Christ and His work. To try to impose an unvarying pattern, even in one age or country, can only entail divergence and disunity.

Again, the sacraments as means and foci of unity conform to the pattern of death and resurrection which always emerges where there is genuine unity and unification in Christ. Not only do they carry with them a plain call to mortification and renewal. But they themselves are signs destined to pass with the passing of the present aeon, and under a constant process of change in their temporal form and order. To absolutize a particular form of administration, pressing and defending it at all costs and against all comers, is to refuse the essential movement of Christian discipleship and therefore to create and perpetuate disunity. But to accept a genuine reformability under the Word and Spirit, realizing that we can give only a variable and varying form to these enduring actions, is to enter the path of common humility and self-denial on which each can recognize and help even if he cannot always understand or approve the other.

Finally, they conform to the pattern of ministry or service. For the sacraments, like confession and the Bible, are not autonomous, nor are they given us in order that we should assess and judge one another. They are means of grace, i.e., means of attesting Jesus Christ, of proffering Him, both to ourselves and to a needy world. In this ministry the work of the sacraments, though it may be evangelistic as a witness to the world or to the children of believers, is primarily edificatory, serving to sign and seal the faith evoked by the biblical Word and expressed in the confession, and strengthening Christians in the fellowship of faith. But the main point is that ministry is their proper office. They are not designed to be standards of reference, or agencies of rebuttal and division, or the remote seals of lofty human attainment. They are active means for the furtherance of the whole life and unity of the church, binding Christians together in the one faith in the one Lord, in the common holding out of this Lord and His work to the world, and therefore in their common discipleship and ministry.

When we come to the practical application, the two things which the sacraments demand as sacraments of Christ and His work are recognition on the one side and a measure of integration on the other. When their true nature is seen, it is obvious that anything else is a denial of their proper being and work, and prevents them from exercising to its full extent their true function as means and foci of the unity which we have by faith in Christ and which we have to express to the world. Though the detailed problems differ, in the case of both sacraments there are obstacles both to recognition and integration; and in view of basic similarity of the problem and its solution we may treat them together in this necessarily brief survey.

Recognition means the acceptance of baptisms and communions administrated, however imperfectly, in genuine obedience to the command of Christ and fulfillment of His institution. It carries with it a threefold corollary: first, that the baptized will be recognized as such and no attempt made to repeat their baptism; second, that where circumstances require, communion may be enjoyed at any administration; and third, that communion will be administered to any baptized and confessing member of any other church. The obstacles opposed are of two main classes. In the first place, it may be objected that there is a deficiency in the mode or perhaps the understanding, as, for example, when Baptists argue that without immersion or a conscious expression of faith there is no true baptism. Second, it is claimed that certain other things are necessary to what is not very biblically distinguished as a regular or valid sacrament, e.g., an episcopally ordained minister or communicants who are confirmed according to a particular if not necessarily episcopal form. In these cases it will be seen that a measure of detailed integration of belief and practice is regarded as necessary to recognition; that the sacrament is thus suspended from its unificatory office; and that it becomes a subject of practical or dogmatic contention instead of itself a means of integration.

But why should recognition come first, and how is it to be achieved? It should come first because, as we have seen, sacraments are primarily sacraments of Christ, because in virtue of their "incarnational" character they may as the same sacraments take many legitimate and very varied forms, because they are always subject to criticism and reformation in outward administration and understanding, and because they are instituted as part of the ministry of service. To demand a prior integration is to offend against all these basic principles, to isolate the subsidiary foci from the primary, to impose a new pattern of unity, and even to suspend the sacraments themselves upon other factors. The actual attainment of recognition is simple once a true understanding is achieved and the spiritual challenge is accepted. Baptists, for example, may still feel that theirs is the true way, but on this basis they cannot deny that others are giving a sacrament of Christ and His work, and therefore genuine if imperfect baptism. Similarly, Baptist administrations may be fully accepted as a legitimate variation with a real lesson in the emphasis upon the need for conscious decision. Again, Episcopalians may insist that there is a real and even necessary value in the orderly succession of ministry maintained by a form of episcopacy, but against this background they cannot deny that non-Episcopalians are in their own way administering a sacrament of Christ in obedience to His command, and therefore doing that in which they can basically join them for all the reservations that they might have in this or that respect.

A short word might be included at this point on the specific issues of re-baptism and inter-communion. As regards the first, Baptists have to learn two lessons if they are to make the contribution which they might to practical unification in orientation on the one baptism (Eph. 4:5). They have to learn that baptism is basically the sacrament of Christ and His work, not of me and mine; so that baptism itself stands even though my own response may yet be lacking, or, if I am an adult, insincere. And they have also to learn that in their baptismal teaching and practice they are called to genuine evangelism and edification, not to contention and propaganda. On the other side, the more traditional churches have been slow to recognize that what Baptists do is real baptism even though its theology may be one-sided, but willingly to concede to them this particular form and humbly to accept the genuine lesson which it carries.

In respect of inter-communion, it is sometimes argued that this is the goal of practical unification. But if they are really to achieve unification in orientation on the one cup (I Cor. 10:21), those who speak in this way have also to learn two lessons: first, that unity is already the true actuality of the church in Christ; and second, that the one cup is a means to its practical expression. To perpetuate a divided cup is both to deny that the body is really one until we make it so, and to turn one of the means and foci of unity into its opposite. To be sure, inter-communion is not to be abused either by the uneasy flitting from table to table or its prostitution as a mere manifesto. Nor is it to be regarded as a substitute for the genuine effort at integration which is demanded between denominational churches in the one country or locality. But the fact remains that on the basis of the true unity of the church, and in accordance with its necessary pattern, there can be no justification for its refusal.

When unity is believed and accepted, recognition of the sacraments of others is obviously the first step. But when it is seen that faith must issue in obedience, there can be no evading the task of integration. This is the case even between different territorial churches, for while it is true that these may follow different paths of practice and formulation in response to different outlooks or circumstances, they cannot do so in isolation, as if what they did in their sphere were of no concern to what others do in other spheres. Even between national church groupings there is thus a need for constant discussion in which each can learn from the successes and failures of the other under the common lordship of the Word and Spirit. But if this is true of national churches, it is even more true of the denominational churches engaged in competitive and perhaps widely divergent sacramental administration in the one country and town and even village. Recognition, especially in the form of inter-communion, is a first step, but it is not the last; for in the one place it still leaves the scandal of the two or many cups, not legitimately of different congregations of the one church, but illegitimately of different and to that extent, even though the relations may be ever so cordial and harmonious, competitive churches. By mutual recognition the sacraments are freed to do their positive work. And since unity is part of this work, they necessarily demand a concretion in definite integration.

This involves two definite stages. First, there is required the attainment of a definite structure of unity in the one locality so that all the churches, even though their sacramental practice and beliefs may vary, are congregations of the one church. Only then is there really achieved the concretion of the one cup, and the consequent growing together in all other branches of Christian life and work. But, second, there is also required a patient examination of the various sacramental modes and practices and tenets, not with a view to the enforcement of a new uniformity, but for mutual assimilation and enrichment and for the softening of more glaring or harmful anomalies or discrepancies. In this respect caution is needed. Administrators often love a lowest common denominator, quenching the true movement of reformation and renewal by the imposition of the unimaginatively mediocre, and preventing the work of genuine edification by failing to allow for legitimate diversity. In the one church, the congregations with their diverse forms of outlook and worship must be encouraged to grow together in order that new and richer and more powerful forms may emerge under the guidance of the Word and impulsion of the Spirit. But they must really grow. They must not be squeezed into an ecclesiastical mold. Thus adult baptism may still flourish alongside infant; immersion alongside affusion; liturgical and more ornate forms alongside the more simple and spontaneous; the one Spirit exercising His diverse gifts in the one church according to His manifold distribution (I Cor. 12:4ff.) and thus causing it, not to be rent asunder or to pursue an independent life in each of its members, but to "come in the unity of the faith, and of the knowledge of the Son of God, unto a perfect man, unto the measure of the stature of the fulness of Christ" (Eph. 4:13).

CHAPTER TWELVE

UNITY AND THE MINISTRY

———

A FINAL MEANS and focus of unity, closely associated with the Bible and sacraments on the one side and confession on the other, is the ministry in its narrower and more specific sense. This was obviously instituted by the Lord for continuing work in the church. He gave a special commission to the diciples (John 20:21), and later to Paul (Gal. 1:15f.). In addition, He sent out seventy others (Luke 10:1ff.), and seems to have given a charge to all the first believers (Luke 24:33.). The deacons, too, although originally set apart for a specific function, seem to have shared in the more general ministry of proclamation, even taking the lead both in Jerusalem and further afield (Acts 6:8ff., 8:26ff.).

The fact that the whole church is engaged in a ministry, and that particular men are called and ordained to particular functions of ministry, is clearly a unifying factor in the life of the church and the churches. The forms of ministry may vary widely from age to age and place to place. The way in which it is exercised may range from the formal and sluggish on the one side to the active and dynamic on the other. The attempt may even be made to dispense with ministers in any professional sense. But the fact remains that, as the church is called to service, it always entails the ministry. In the ministry, therefore, we have both a means and focus of unity.

Yet here again there is the impulse to disunity as well

as unity. This is seen especially in two fields. There are differences in the conception of the work of ministry, whether in respect of the Godward ministry of worship or the manward ministry of preaching and supervision. And there are differences in the structure of the ministry itself, ranging from the larger differences between Papal, Episcopalian, Presbyterian, and Congregational systems, to the smaller differences of arrangement within these systems. In some cases, the differences obviously amount to little more than a legitimate diversity which occasions no great difficulty. In others, however, there is involved a non-recognition of ministry which both creates and perpetuates actual disunion. Indeed, even where there is recognition it may still carry with it a competitiveness which is tantamount to genuine disunion, notwithstanding the affability and occasional cooperativeness which may be displayed.

In this as in other spheres, it must be realized that the ministry, and especially a particular form of the ministry, is not an absolute or independent focus. If it is to be a genuine means of unity, it must be brought into strict relationship to Christ and seen in conformity with the pattern of unity which this entails. The main points to be grasped in this respect may be briefly summarized. First, Christ is the basis and theme of the ministry in the twofold sense that He Himself instituted it and that it exists to praise and proclaim Him. Second, it is ordained for the evoking and strengthening of a common faith in Him and therefore a unity of faith. Third, it reflects again the incarnational duality of Christ and the church, in the sense that ministry as such, which is enduring and even eternal, finds many and changing forms in the temporal historical order. Fourth, it is subject to the law of death and resurrection both as a whole in the mortality of the whole ministry as we now know it, and in detail in the temporary and therefore reformable character of the particular forms which it assumes. Finally, and very obviously, it is not an end in itself, but is caught up in the whole ministry of reconciliation, i.e., the saving action of God Himself in the world. Only when the ministry is seen in this wider context can there be any fruitful use of it as a means and focus of unity instead of disunity.

Before we take up the practical problems, a word may first be said about the actual work of ministry. For here, too, many differences arise which are a potent cause of dissension and schism and aloofness in the churches. From the standpoint of worship, for example, there are many varying forms which particular groups are tempted to absolutize as though theirs were the only pure or possible ministry and there could be no dealings with those who think and act otherwise. From the pastoral standpoint, there are very different approaches which in the last resort may well rest upon doctrinal divergences but which work themselves out in practical suspicion and isolation. From the evangelistic standpoint there are wide strategic and tactical differences which at very least result in non-cooperation and may sometimes involve tragic schisms such as that which separated Anglicanism and Methodism in the eighteenth century.

Now it is clearly just as impossible to achieve and enforce uniformity in these and other forms of service as it is to achieve and enforce uniformity in the sphere of detailed doctrine. Ministry itself remains, and by and large will manifest itself along common lines. For instance, there will be worship, preaching, teaching, and practical help. Worship itself will fall into the general categories of praise, confession, prayer, reading, preaching, and sacramental administration. Preaching and teaching will take recognized forms, as will also practical help (e.g., medical care, general education, visitation, and relief of the poor and needy). But along these common lines and within these general categories we have to recognize that there may be many forms, each with a relative justification, each supplementing or instructing the other, but each subject to the searching and purifying action of the Word and Spirit. The pursuit of a uniform absolute, whether in terms of scriptural precedent or historical tradition or past experience, can only lead to disruption and the hampering of the true work of ministry. To be sure, the lessons of the past must be studied in the forms which we shape and use, and whatever is done must be brought under the ultimate norm of Scripture. But place is still left for very wide variety in the detailed practice of ministry, not only in different ages and localities, but even in the one age and locality; and care must be taken not to quench the moving of the Spirit or to jeopardize the effective prosecution of the ministry for the sake of a fictional absolute or the arrogant assumption that our own is the best and even the only way.

If this is true of the work of ministry, it is just as true of the ministry itself as a separate function within the general ministry of the church. There seems to be little doubt, not only from the general action of the church, but from the New Testament itself and the dominical and apostolic action, that there ought to be this special function of ministry, whatever detailed forms it may take. There seems to be no doubt also that, whatever practical structure may be adopted, it must conform to the three categories of ministry which we meet with in the Bible itself and every age of the church. Some form of supervision or episcopacy must obviously be exercised. There must be an administration of Word and sacrament. And there ought to be a form of diaconate in the narrower sense, the application of temporal resources to the church's ministry. In other words, there are enduring features of ministry which are clearly essential to its proper exercise no matter what may be the conditions or the arrangements used to meet these conditions. To say this, however, is not at all to say that the ministry must take an absolute form, e.g., in the so-called threefold ministry or historical episcopate, and that in default of this detailed form it cannot be accepted as a valid ministry of the church.

On the contrary, both the New Testament and the later

history of the church seem to make it perfectly plain that these functions can be carried out in very different ways, and that different and reformable ways are even demanded in response to varying situations. Even where the threefold structure is retained, the practical exercise and inward relationships can take the most diverse forms which in some cases involve the almost complete failure genuinely to fulfill the allotted functions (cf. the feudal bishops and the modern Anglican diaconate). But the functions themselves can also be fulfilled in different ways even where the historic structure is not maintained, e.g., when a presbytery exercises a corporate superintendence over the life and ministry of the church. It may rightly be insisted that the enduring functions should in fact be fulfilled. The way in which they are fulfilled, however, is a matter for individual historical and geographical groups to fix for themselves in obedience to the Word and Spirit, with a proper sense of responsibility to other historical and geographical groups and with a constant willingness to subject the arrangements made to scrutiny and revision according to historical requirement or biblical direction.

For the practical unifying of the church and its ministry, this means that there is required the same twofold step of recognition and integration which we have already discussed in relation to the sacraments. Between national churches, the task is easier, for even though the form adopted may be deplored or regarded as defective the right of the church to take it cannot be so readily contested. Denominational ministries within the same country pose a more difficult problem, for whatever the rights and wrongs of the original dispute the setting up of a competitive ministry has involved a clear breach of order. However, nothing is gained by legalistic contention. In the given circumstances of the day we can only accept the fact that for better or worse these different ministries exist, and where they are committed to the true task of ministry and fulfill its proper functions we cannot wait for an integrated uniformity which will never come to accord them recognition as true if sometimes rather irregular ministries of Christ.

The apostolic succession calls for consideration in this connection. If it is thought and taught that episcopal ordination in this so-called succession is an absolute requirement for true ministry, or even that there can be no true ministry except where a historic form of the episcopate has been preserved, the problem of recognition becomes insoluble, and there can be a united and unifying ministry only by the imposition and acceptance of a particular form. But is not this to absolutize what is relative and flaunt it against that which is genuinely enduring? Is it not to make a confusion between the genuine apostolic ministry and a relative historical continuity in apostolic derivation, between genuine episcopacy and a particular outworking and exercise in the episcopate? This is not to say that there is no value in an orderly succession or the traditional episcopate. There is so much value that they must be taken into serious account in any movements of integration, and have their own contribution to make by way of positive unification. But they must not be accorded the false and distorted value of a pretended absolute which leads to the overlooking of other forms of the genuine absolute, hinders the processes of scrutiny and reformation, and blocks the way to any true unification.

Recognition, however, is not enough. It must also be accompanied by integration. This is true even of the national churches. For one thing, they do not live in self-containment, but overlap even within their own frontiers and particularly in the wider tasks of the church. For another, they have much to learn from one another for the fuller and more effective discharge of the common functions of ministry. It is even more true of the denominational churches within a single country. Recognition points the way to unity and makes possible a wider and deeper cooperation in many spheres of ministry. But it leaves untouched the basic denial of unity in the existence of competitive ministries. And it does not allow of the enrichment of ministry which might come from integration. It is thus essential that recognition should not be an isolated or even a preliminary move, but that it should be accompanied at once by cooperation on an ever-widening front and discussions and proposals with a view to mutual assimilation. It need hardly be said that the variation of forms makes this a task of no little difficulty. The temptation must be avoided merely to arrive at an artificial compromise. Nor must the matter be left to ecclesiastical legalists or bureaucrats. Nor should there be an unnecessary pursuit of uniformity or finality. The integration must come, as it can and should, out of the enduring functions which are greater than the relative forms in which they now find their varied expression. The fact that there are these functions is the guarantee that an integrated ministry is possible for all the difficulties. It is also a summons to the task, and an indication of the way in which it must be acomplished.

It must be remembered, however, that integration of the ministry is not merely for the sake of a unified ministry, or for the furtherance of the practical unity of the church, but for the concentration of the church upon the common task of ministry which it has in virtue of its one being in Christ. It is one of the more hopeful aspects of modern ecumenicism that it stems from a deep-seated anxiety that divided Christendom cannot properly fulfill its great commission of evangelism either at home or abroad. The artificial spur of competition is no substitute for the impulsion of concerted effort. The danger, of course, is that a mere alliance will be made for the sake of various practical advantages, e.g., in the elimination of waste and better strategic planning. This is right enough in its place. But behind this there is needed something deeper. There is needed the unity in ministry which comes from a knowledge that we are presenting the one Christ to the world in fulfillment of the one commission and for the attainment of the one salvation. A unified ministry is certainly a means and focus of the general unity of the church as this is rooted and grounded in Christ Himself. But it is supremely adapted to be what the other means and foci are also in their different ways, namely, a means and focus of its unity in service. A disunited ministry denies and hampers, though it cannot destroy, this unity. A united ministry not only confirms it but facilitates its practical expression, and in so doing is a powerful factor in the realization of that unity in Christ which is the new and true and eternal reality of His people.

INDEX

INDEX OF SCRIPTURE PASSAGES

INDEX OF SUBJECTS